371.3SS

This book is to be returned
the l...

HOW TO SUCCEED
IN EXAMS AND
ASSESSMENTS

LEARNING SKILLS SERIES

HOW TO SUCCEED IN EXAMS AND ASSESSMENTS

Penny Henderson

Published by
CollinsEducational Ltd
77-85 Fulham Palace Road
Hammersmith
London W6 8JB

First published in 1993
Reprinted 1995

The National Extension College (NEC) is an educational trust with a distinguished body of trustees. Since it was established in 1963, it has pioneered the development of flexible learning for adults. NEC is actively developing innovative materials and systems for distance learning on over 100 courses, from basic skills to degree and professional training. Working in partnership with CollinsEducational, NEC can now offer the best in flexible learning materials to the widest possible audience and further its aim of extending educational opportunities for all.

About the author:

Penny Henderson has written several books on teaching, learning, and groupwork for the National Extension College. She has worked as an Open University tutor for 20 years, and has run groups for students who panic, and trained other tutors to run them. She has worked as a trainer for social services, and freelance as a management consultant and trainer. She now combines counselling work with teaching and writing.

The publishers wish to thank Tim Burton for his invaluable editorial expertise.

British Library Cataloguing-in-Publication Data
A catalogue record for
this book is
available from the
British Library.

ISBN 0 00 322346 9

Typeset by Squires Graphics. Cover design by Information Design Workshop. Printed in Great Britain at Redwood Books, Trowbridge, Wiltshire.

Contents

INTRODUCTION

What is this book about?

Being assessed puts pressure on most people. We want to perform to our full potential, so even when we feel ready and able to do what is being assessed, the process of submitting a sample of work for judgement makes us feel stretched and put on the spot.

This book explores a variety of assessment methods currently in use. It aims to help you to prepare for your particular assessment, and to offer guidance on some useful ways to approach the process. It emphasises that to do well in assessment you need to be clear:

■   what is being assessed;

■   how you are to go about the assessment task;

■   what is an acceptable standard of performance.

It is also useful to become aware of how you respond to being assessed.

What level does the book aim at?

This book is designed to help people being assessed whatever their subject, at whatever level they are being assessed. The principles of approaching assessment are common to the different forms and levels of assessment. So you may be doing any of the following:

■   National Vocational Qualifications (NVQs) or Scottish Vocational Qualifications (SVQs) assessments in college or the workplace;

■   traditional exams;

■   essays or projects or compiling portfolios of work;

■   practical exams to test your skill.

How to use the book

You may be studying it in one of a number of ways:

■   You may have bought the book from a book shop or borrowed it from the library, and plan to work through it on your own.

■   You may be a student on a course, full time or part time, who has been advised to look at it by yourself or with other students to prepare for being assessed.

■   You may be approaching an exam or S/NVQ assessment (in college or your workplace) and your assessor may have recommended it to you.

The book is intended to be used flexibly. As it concerns a variety of assessment methods you are likely to find some units more helpful than others. I recommend that everyone works through Units 2 and 3 before going on to other units. But if you are about to be assessed, you may want to look through it quickly and then turn to units that you feel are particularly relevant.

If you plan to work through the book systematically, then it will take about 30 to 50 hours spread over some time. This is just a guide: people work at different speeds so don't worry if you take more or less time.

How is the book organised?

This is not a traditional textbook. It is designed to help you learn in an active way, and to apply the ideas to your own situation. So I have included some special features.

Self-Assessment Questions (SAQs)

SAQs are indicated by this symbol. These may be opportunities for you to:

■ check what you have learned;

■ apply the ideas discussed to your own situation;

■ draw up a plan of action in response to the ideas in the workbook.

Most SAQs do not have 'right' answers, only the answer that is right for you. But I will aim to explore the types of response I would expect to find. If I do not include yours it may mean no more than that I failed to think of it!

We recommend that you use a sheet of A4 paper or card to cover the text beneath an SAQ to stop yourself reading the answer before you have written down your own.

What this unit is about

Each of the subsequent units in this book begins with this heading. 'What this unit is about' outlines what the unit contains. You can use this to decide whether or not you want to work through the unit.

What other books are needed to work through this book?

This book is self-contained. It is intended to help you to prepare effectively for the assessment which forms part of your course or study programme. You will also find it helpful to have information about the content of your course: the syllabus and assessment requirements. Use this book to identify how you can best prepare for your course assessments, and then put your energy into applying the ideas while you study your course.

Using other resources

This book encourages you to take stock of the resources available to you for your assessment. Some of these are practical: you can collect information about the syllabus, examiners' reports, and criteria for assessment, as suggested in Unit 3. The rest are human: your tutor and any other students, and those who care for you, and wish to support you and help you to succeed. Unit 11 encourages you to consider revising with other students, if they are willing.

UNIT 2

UNDERSTANDING ASSESSMENT

What this unit is about

In this unit you will look at what assessment is, and at the different types of assessment people are faced with. It will help you understand and describe the assessment process you are going through.

By the time you finish your work on this unit you should be able to:

→ identify the difference between informal and formal assessment;

→ describe formative and summative assessment;

→ state what is meant by norm referenced assessment and criterion referenced assessment;

→ describe the assessment structure you will be going through.

The unit includes explanations of several terms commonly used to describe assessment. You may find it useful to refer back to these when you are working through later units.

What is assessment?

Being assessed involves being judged. This happens in everyday life as well as to students. Taking part in a swimming competition and being interviewed for a new job both involve some form of assessment.

1 Write down up to four activities you have carried out recently that have involved some sense of assessment. (You may have been the assessor or the assessed.) Read on only after you have noted down your answer.

The possibilities I thought of include:

- taking a driving test;
- taking an exam;
- being involved in an appraisal at work;
- going out with a new date;
- joining a committee;
- preparing a report for work.

These are varied experiences and form different types of assessment. Assessments may be informal or formal, and they may be formative or summative.

Informal assessment

Most assessment is informal, and we so take it for granted that we are barely aware it is happening or that everyone takes part in the process.

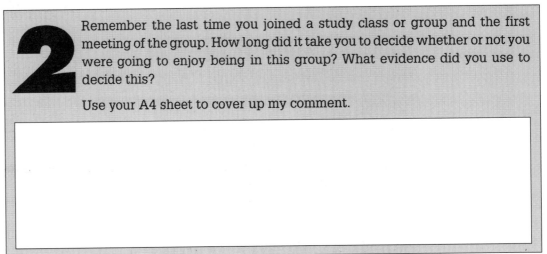

Remember the last time you joined a study class or group and the first meeting of the group. How long did it take you to decide whether or not you were going to enjoy being in this group? What evidence did you use to decide this?

Use your A4 sheet to cover up my comment.

By the end of the first meeting you may have an idea whether or not you are going to enjoy being in a group. A number of factors are likely to influence such an impression, such as the tutor's manner, use of first names, opportunities to participate and atmosphere in the group. These are all criteria for your informal assessment of your new group. You may also agree that this initial informal assessment may often need to be revised later on.

In the same way, tutors informally assess by observation the students whom they teach. They notice who is alert; who answers class questions; who is punctual in submitting work; who approaches assessment confidently. They too may need to amend an early impression and check their informal assessment against a more systematic and formal process in order to be fair and just.

Formal assessment

Formal assessments are recognised assessment 'events'. They include exams, tests, quizzes, practical demonstrations, presentations, essays, projects, journals and portfolios. Students need to know what will be assessed, when the work is due and/or when the assessment will take place.

In a formal assessment the assessors use the same basis for judging the performance of all the candidates taking part in it. In this way formal assessments try to be fair to everyone.

Any formal assessment is in danger of assessing what it is easy to measure, and can only assess a fraction of what the students have learned. But on the other hand informal assessments are at risk of personal bias, and are seldom done systematically. They need to be supplemented with formal assessments.

Some formal assessments, such as exams, practical demonstrations and presentations, also ensure that an assessor is judging the candidate's own unaided work.

3 Here are four assessment situations. Note beside each one whether it is formal or informal.

Don't forget to use your A4 sheet.

- joining a new group;

- taking a driving test;

- meeting your partner's parents or good friends for the first time;

- writing an essay.

You will probably agree with me that the first and third situations are informal, but the second and fourth are formal.

Formative assessment

In a formative assessment your assessor will judge your performance, and then give you information about how well you did. These comments allow you to review your learning.

Formative assessments provide you with opportunities to practise what you have learned, with the intention of improving your performance in the next assessment.

Summative assessment

Summative assessments count towards a final grade or the qualification you are working towards. They tend to be formal assessment events, and may have the same variety of formats as formal assessments. So, for instance, they could be exams, essays, projects, portfolios, journals and tests, or observations of your practical or written work. Some courses include some informal assessment, such as observation of your participation on the course, as part of the whole summative assessment.

While the purpose of formative assessment is to give you information about how you are tackling a task, the purpose of summative assessment is to inform others as well as yourself about the standard of your work.

Summative assessment can take place at intervals during the course (known as continuous assessment) and at the end of a programme of study (final assessment). Many courses these days have a combination of continuous and final assessment.

What is the basis on which candidates are to be judged?

There are two main systems for assessing people:

■ norm referenced systems, where candidates are compared against one another;

■ criterion referenced systems, where candidates are each compared against an accepted standard.

For example, in a high-jump competition the people taking part all compete, and as the height gradually rises they drop out when they can't jump the new height. The final scores and rank order then show each participant's performance in relation to everyone else's. This is a norm referenced system. It is inevitable that some will fail in relation to others.

In criterion referenced assessment the high jump is set at a certain height – 1.7 metres, for instance – and everyone who can jump this height gains the same recognition. Here each participant's performance is compared against a clear standard to be reached. All those who meet the standard pass the test and are declared competent. We look in more detail at criterion referenced assessment in Unit 3.

4 Identify whether the following describe formative or summative assessments and whether they are norm referenced or criterion referenced.

	Formative	Summative	Norm referenced	Criterion referenced
1 A multiple-choice questionnaire to diagnose what you do not yet know, before starting work on a course or topic.	☐	☐	☐	☐
2 A test to see where you stand in comparison to others doing the course with you.	☐	☐	☐	☐
3 A practical demonstration to show whether you can do a certain task in the way required by your organisation.	☐	☐	☐	☐

You will probably agree with my response:

1 Formative – criterion referenced.

2 Summative – norm referenced.

3 Summative – criterion referenced.

5 Note down two or three formal assessments you have been involved in. (You may like to look back at the list you made in SAQ 1 to see if any are appropriate.)

Beside each one note whether they were formative or summative, criterion referenced or norm referenced.

Here are some suggestions I thought of:

■ taking my driving test: summative, criterion referenced;

■ competing in a swimming gala: summative, norm referenced;

■ doing a mock exam, or practice exam: formative, could be either norm referenced or criterion referenced depending on the purpose of the exam;

■ the portfolio I put together for my Counselling Diploma. All candidates had to choose material to include under the same headings, but there was no ranking of candidates and we each either passed or failed the course as a whole. This is summative and criterion referenced assessment.

You should now be able to identify whether an assessment is formal or informal, formative or summative, and whether it is based on a norm referenced system or a criterion referenced system. These descriptions are useful when it comes to understanding the assessment process you are going through. I look next at your assessment structure. In Unit 3 I focus on what is to be assessed and the basis of the assessment.

Your own assessment structure

When you enrol on a course or prepare for assessment at work or in college it is useful to become familiar with the structure of your assessment. This involves finding the answers to the following questions:

1   What form does the assessment take?

2   When does assessment take place?

3   Who assesses your work?

Look at one woman's description of a history course she took at school:

In my history course I was expected to hand in a number of essays – one every two weeks or so. These were marked by my teacher and he would write comments and suggestions in the margin. While I was working on the course I also had to do two pieces of extended work – in the first year I did a project on the history of a castle in our county, and in the second I wrote a long essay about Elizabethan times. These were assessed by an examiner at the examinations board. At the end of the course I took an exam.

From this description you can see that the course contained both formative and summative assessment, and the summative assessment was a combination of continuous and final assessments.

The student could have described the assessment structure of her course as follows:

Assessment type:	How?	When?	By whom?
Formative	essays	throughout the course	teacher
Summative	project long essay exam	first year second year end of course	examiner/assessor examiner/assessor examiner/assessor

You may find it useful to consider the assessment structure of your own course. If you have any material that describes or introduces it, you may find that it contains details of the types of assessment on the course. If not, you may like to find out about the assessment structure from your tutor.

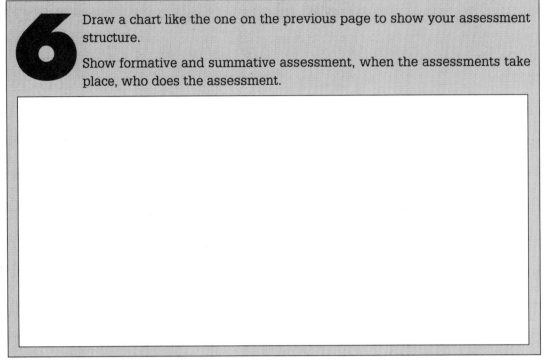

Draw a chart like the one on the previous page to show your assessment structure.

Show formative and summative assessment, when the assessments take place, who does the assessment.

You may find it helpful to build on the notes in your chart by answering the following questions:

- What form does the formative assessment take: for instance, essays, assignments, tests, practice demonstrations, presentations?

- What form does the summative assessment take: for instance, essays, assignments, tests, demonstrations, presentations, exams, portfolios, journals?

- How many pieces of work make up the summative assessment?

- When precisely do the assessments take place? (Be as specific as you can.)

- How far are you to be assessed by your course tutor, who knows you personally?

- How far are you to be assessed by people who have not taught you (for example, examiners)?

- Do other students have a role as assessors?

- What part does your own assessment of your progress play?

Summary

In this unit you have explored the following terms:

- informal and formal assessment;

- formative and summative assessment;

- norm referenced and criterion referenced assessment.

You have also looked at the structure of your assessment process.

The next unit focuses on the process of your assessment by looking further at what is to be assessed and how you will be assessed.

UNIT 3 FINDING OUT WHAT YOUR ASSESSOR IS LOOKING FOR

What this unit is about

Unit 2 asked you to draw a chart to show the structure of assessment for your course or study programme. This unit helps you to clarify precisely what the assessment involves.

By the time you finish this unit you should be able to:

➔ describe the knowledge, skills and attitudes required in your assessment;

➔ identify the basis on which you will be judged.

If your assessment includes an exam you should also be able to:

➔ describe the structure of your exam;

➔ explain what an examiner is hoping to find in an exam paper;

➔ anticipate the kinds of common mistakes you might make in an exam.

What is being assessed?

If you are preparing for assessment it is worth being clear about precisely what your assessor or examiner is looking for. The syllabus is a key document used by assessors as it specifies what candidates are expected to know, so I suggest you become familiar with your syllabus, course brochure or similar course documentation.

Syllabuses are not always easy to understand, so it is worth setting aside enough time to look at yours.

Your syllabus or equivalent document should tell you:

■ the aims of the course of study;

■ what you should be able to do on completion of the course;

■ the structure of the assessment;

■ the detailed content of the course.

As a first step it is worth finding out:

■ What knowledge is required?

■ What skills are being tested?

■ Does the assessment include monitoring of your attitudes or personal approach?

Knowledge

Your syllabus should make clear whether the focus of the assessment is on correctly recalling the facts, or on using facts to present an argument. Syllabuses often include lists of books that you need to read, and specify the key ideas or information you will need to grasp.

Skills

The skills tested by assessment may be social, practical, intellectual or creative. These may be assessed through practical demonstrations, performance or preparation of a portfolio of work. The syllabus may also specify skills in writing or speaking persuasively, in which case you need to be clear whether assessments will take into account presentation skills. For example, will you be given marks for spelling, neatness, grammar, using diagrams or tables?

Attitudes

Your attitude or personal approach is not usually relevant to most academic assessments, but can be a central element in S/NVQ assessments or in course assessments of practical and interpersonal skills.

For instance, students on a hotel course may have to make a bed neatly. Their attitude while making the bed is not significant. But students who are caring for elderly people in hospital may have to make a bed neatly with the person in it, attending to their personal as well as physical needs. In such a case the student's approach and attitudes are clearly important.

1 Choose one section of your syllabus and identify the knowledge, skills and attitudes/behaviour required:

knowledge

skills

attitudes

If possible, check your response with your tutor, a fellow student, or someone who is familiar with your course and assessment process.

What is the basis on which you are to be assessed?

It is helpful to know whether your assessment will be based on a norm referenced system or a criterion referenced system. Unit 2 describes the difference between the two systems, and you may like to read page 11 to review the meaning of the two terms. But first, check your learning with the following SAQ.

Which of the following describes norm referenced assessment, and which describes criterion referenced assessment?

1   A system designed to compare all candidates against an accepted standard:

2   A system designed to compare all candidates against each other:

Many courses and S/NVQs are now clearly and explicitly criterion referenced and students are given – or develop their own – learning objectives to meet the criteria. One by-product of this is that students no longer compete with each other for a rank order of success. Instead they judge their progress against a target, and everyone can pass.

Look at the following example, which is an extract from the standards required for the City and Guilds Certificate in Communication Skills (Wordpower), Stage 1:

Unit 6 Conversing with more than one person

Description

This unit refers to verbal communication with a number of people in work and social contexts where a degree of formality is required. It deals with arrivals and departures and providing information.

ELEMENT 2 Provide information to more than one person

Range

Giving a short talk or presentation, either free-standing or within a meeting or other group occasion. The input should be on one main issue and last for around five minutes. The group should be of between three and six people who are not likely to undermine the candidate's confidence and should act in a responsive manner.

Example activities

Showing people around a club. office or sports ground; showing potential buyers or tenants around a house; giving a briefing to colleagues on the priorities for a day's work; talking about a particular interest.

(continued overleaf)

ASSESSMENT SCHEDULE

In at least two real or simulated situations of the type illustrated in the range the candidate must demonstrate that he/she can:

PERFORMANCE CRITERIA

2.1 explain clearly to audience/group the scope and range of information to be provided

2.2 present information in a sensible order

2.3 use appropriate volume, tone of voice, articulation, body language and facial expression for situation/audience/group

2.4 encourage and answer questions from the group

2.5 provide further sources of help or information, if unable to answer a question.

Both assessors and candidates use the information in this extract to find out precisely:

- what needs to be assessed (a short talk or presentation);
- how often it needs to be assessed (two real or simulated situations);
- the way a candidate should carry out the activities (performance criteria).

Find out whether your assessment is norm referenced or criterion referenced by looking at your syllabus, assessment scheme or course documentation, or by talking to your tutor.

Whether your assessment is norm referenced, or criterion referenced, it is not always easy to be clear about what precisely is required. Give yourself time and if possible discuss your understanding with your tutor, a fellow student, or someone you know who has been through the same assessment process.

What does your examiner expect?

This section is essential reading for exam candidates. If you are not taking an exam as part of your assessment you may find it useful to skim through it.

The structure of the exam

In exams you need to focus your energy on gaining the maximum marks you can for each question in the time you have available. It is a bit like playing Scrabble competitively: you go for a word which gives you a high score, rather than a satisfyingly unusual word which scores fewer points! In order to plan for the exam you need to know the rules: what the exam consists of, the questions you can expect to find, how the marks are allocated. Again your syllabus or course information should give you details, but if it doesn't ask your tutor.

Answer the following questions to identify the structure of your exam. Write your answers on a separate sheet of paper if necessary.

■ How many papers will there be?

■ What percentage of the marks does each paper carry?

■ Must you pass all papers?

For each paper:

■ How much time do you have to sit the paper?

■ What sort of questions will there be? (Essays, short-answer questions, case studies, multiple-choice?)

■ How many questions must you answer?

■ Which questions, if any, are compulsory?

■ Which questions, if any, are optional?

■ How are marks allocated?

■ How does the content of the paper relate to the syllabus?

Look at old exam papers, or specimen papers specially written for a new course. These will give you a sense of the way the exam will be set out.

How to find out what the examiner is looking for

Examiners are not setting out to trick you when they set an exam. Their aim is to design questions that enable you to demonstrate your knowledge of the subject and ability to write about it. They want to see if you have understood the questions you attempt, can include relevant information and have a grasp of the subject. The best exam questions allow able candidates to show their ability, while those who should earn a bare pass can still answer at their own level.

There are several sources of information to help you identify what examiners are looking for.

Mark schemes

Many published syllabuses now include a general mark scheme in which the examiner describes the qualities of a typical answer at each grade.

It is less common for the mark scheme of a particular exam to be published, but you may be able to see one.

Examiners' reports

Most exam boards publish a detailed report after each exam is complete and the results are finalised. These contain helpful summaries of common faults and difficulties, together with accounts of good answers, often question by question, and quoting examples taken from actual answers.

Past papers

In the case of a new exam, specimen papers will be published with the syllabus. Do NOT use specimen papers or past papers to question-spot, but do use them to get an idea of what kinds of questions are asked, as a source of titles for practice answers, and as a way to familiarise yourself with the structure of the exam as a whole.

Model answers

Though many of these are published, my advice to you is to avoid them. At best, they tell you the answers to last year's exam; at worst, they are positively misleading.

5 Find out what documentation is available from your exam board or awarding body – and how much they cost. You could write to your awarding body or ask your tutor.

Note the addresses and phone numbers below:

If you are studying with other students, you could send in a bulk order at the beginning of the course which you can then share.

Common failings reported by examiners

The following is a list of the most common reasons cited in examiners' reports for students failing to gain marks.

1   Failing to answer the question.

2   Failing to recognise the meaning of specialist or technical terms that are central to the understanding of the course material, or failing to demonstrate understanding of them by defining them.

3   Failing to write answers in the form required. For example, if you are asked to make a case for or against something, the examiner will give you few marks if you put down what you know about it but do not say what your position is on it.

4   Failing to use the course material as evidence in your answer; using personal anecdotes instead of reasoned answers.

5   Failing to use the course material discriminatingly by selecting the most relevant ideas to answer the question.

6   Failing to put appropriate time aside for each question, so that later ones are answered in a rush and are scrappy or non-existent.

7   Failing to follow the exam paper's instructions about how many or which questions to answer, or to answer all parts of a question.

8   Illegible handwriting. (This is not always penalised, though it usually makes examiners extremely grumpy!)

9   Failing to check for very obvious mistakes, such as simple mathematical errors, or historical dates in completely the wrong century.

10   Writing long, complex, unclear sentences.

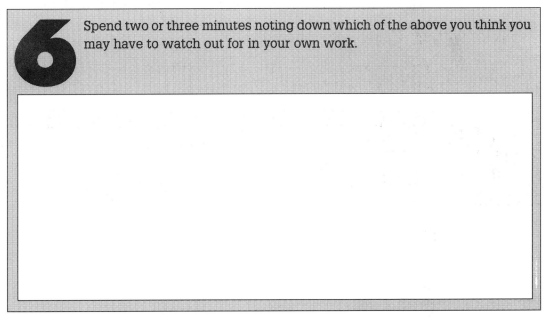

Spend two or three minutes noting down which of the above you think you may have to watch out for in your own work.

You may find it difficult to anticipate whether you will have any of the problems listed above. If this is the case, you may like to find out whether you can do a mock, or practice, exam, which your tutor can mark and give you comments on under each of the points in the above list.

Note that many of the common failings listed above are to do with exam technique rather than knowledge and competence in the subject being examined.

The list highlights the need for candidates to:

- prepare thoroughly for an exam – **Units 5, 10** and **11**;

- build on comments from tutors during the coursework – **Unit 6**;

- control anxiety – **Unit 9**;

- control the urge for perfectionism – **Unit 8**;

- focus on what the question is asking – **Unit 12**;

- pace themselves during the exam – **Unit 13**.

You may want to look particularly at the units that seem most relevant to you.

Examiners are human too

Some students picture their examiner as a hawk waiting to pounce on every error, or a harsh teacher, or bewigged judge, or grey-haired academic in mortarboard and gown. It is important to remind yourself that your examiner is unlikely to be a cold, stern, judgemental figure who will spend hours searching for your every mistake. Rather, imagine them marking a lot of scripts quickly to meet a very tight schedule, and for very little pay per script. See them as human beings: their baby may have kept them up during the night; they may be anxious to complete their marking to their deadline. They need all the help you can give them by legible handwriting, short sentences, and clear layout, so they can identify every mark you have earned.

Summary

In this unit I have encouraged you to become familiar with your course syllabus or other similar document so that you know what your assessor will expect you to be able to do when you come to an assessment.

If you are taking an exam you should have a clearer idea of how your exam is structured, what your examiner is looking for and how to find out more information about this, and some of the common mistakes students make in exams.

Knowing what your assessments involve is an important stage in preparing for them. But it is also useful to consider how you feel about being assessed. I look at this in the next unit.

UNIT 4

SELF-REVIEW

What this unit is about

This unit looks at an aspect of assessment that is all too easy to overlook: the feelings that it generates in you. These feelings, and the way you cope with them, may be a critical factor in your success.

By the time you have finished your work on this unit you should be able to:

➜ describe how you feel about being assessed;

➜ describe what motivates you to do your course;

➜ identify sources of self-confidence which may affect your attitude to being assessed.

What motivates you?

Student motivation is usually mixed: some is extrinsic, to do with gaining qualifications, recognition and rewards; some is intrinsic, to do with the inherent pleasure, interest and delight of learning. You are responsible for creating your own strategy for getting the best out of the course for your own needs. It is useful, then, to identify your reasons for studying, so that you are more aware of what is rewarding to you. For example, do you get most satisfaction when you imagine yourself having gained the qualification, or when you imagine yourself knowing what you do not know yet?

This SAQ will help you analyse your motives for doing your course or study programme and to identify what helps you sustain your enjoyment in learning.

1   Are you doing the course mainly to learn all you can about this subject? If you are, what most helps you to do this?

(continued overleaf)

2   Are you doing the course mainly to get a qualification? If so, what will you do to ensure you do gain it?

3   For what other reasons are you doing the course? (For example, is it to pass the time because there are no jobs available?) Is this a good strategy which is paying off for you?

What is important is that you find ways to keep up your own motivation. Your tutor may play an important part in this.

How your tutor can help

Tutors who assume all students are there for the love of learning may offer different rewards and incentives from those who assume they are there just to get a qualification at the end. If your tutor's expectations of you differ from your own, you may find that what is intended to be encouragement grates on you. You may find it helpful to talk to your tutor about your own reasons for studying and discuss how he or she can help increase your motivation. For example, could your tutor comment more fully on certain aspects of your work? Could she or he provide more information about the assessment process?

How do you feel about being assessed?

Your motivation is likely to affect your approach to assessment. For example, if a qualification is important to you, you may feel a rush of anxiety just thinking about being assessed. Even if you are highly motivated to do well in your assessment, your attitudes are likely to be influenced by past experience.

So as you prepare for assessment, it's relevant and useful to review your earlier experiences of the process. This will help you to clarify how you feel about your forthcoming assessment.

For instance, most people who had bad experiences in school exams are affected by these when they approach later assessments. Unsuccessful or traumatic experiences of learning to read, or of taking tests and exams at school or college, can influence how an individual expects to perform in future assessments.

But people do not respond to bad experiences in the same way. For example, one person may be determined to prove something, and therefore be very highly motivated to succeed in an assessment despite being a bit tense about it, while another may be afraid they will repeat a poor performance and feel scared.

If, on the other hand, you are one of the fortunate people who can say: 'I've always done well in exams, perhaps better than I deserve' you will begin from a completely different point: optimistic, and confident in your expectations.

Make a list of some of the significant experiences of assessment you can easily recall in five minutes.

You could include exams taken at different ages, aiming for particular standards of achievement at sports (swimming a particular distance; running at a particular speed), music, drama or a skill.

Beside each, note how you feel about it now and how your experience affects your expectations about being assessed.

My list (with some pruning!) looks like this:

- Swam 50 metres when I was 7, and got certificate. Felt very pleased because my mother was a champion swimmer, and I thought I could be too. I am still a keen swimmer, though not a competitive one, and I always smile when I find the old certificate in the bottom of my documents box.

- Took and passed 11-plus. The teacher at the primary school had been very cruel and dismissive about my messy writing, so I can remember feeling quite anxious that I would fail and it would be all because of this. I still dislike critical comments about my writing.

- Got a distinction in a drama exam at 15: I was particularly delighted as I had to work very hard to get one particular piece right and in the end I had my highest mark for that bit. I don't now have significant fears about performing in public.

- Failed O level Maths so badly the school would not allow me to take it again, as it would ruin their statistics. I felt convinced before I took it that I was likely to fail, and have avoided any mathematical enterprise since — a severe handicap in everyday life.

- I wasn't interested in taking O level Art because my puny efforts were greeted with 'That's very nice dear, what is it?' or 'You'd better go and try some basket work.' When I was 47 I began mask-making and painting with great anxiety, and with a sense of wonderment and delight when I found myself using paints to express what I wanted to.

In spite of knowing the theory about how damaging a sense of failure can be to people's confidence, I was surprised when I made this list to see how clearly the successes and failures have affected my later choices of what to learn, what to avoid, and what I am confident about.

3 Look back at your list and consider whether your reactions to success and failure are linked as clearly as mine are. Note any comments or observations below.

How do you feel about your capacity to take on your current course of study?

If possible, discuss what you have identified with a friend, fellow student or tutor, especially if you think this may affect your approach to being assessed.

If you are doing a long course, perhaps towards a degree or professional qualification, and part of your assessment requires you to do work which you have found difficult in the past, it is useful to consider whether you still feel uncertain of your ability. I did when I started making masks, for example. On the other hand, you may now be aware that you can do this work well enough to pass an exam on it. It often happens that students who do poorly in a particular subject at school later discover that they are excellent in some very closely related field. If you are in this category, go back over your list to see where you need to build your confidence now.

The following section may help you with this.

Sources of self-confidence

Almost everyone is confident about something that they do, though not all of us are able to say so to others. Relatively few people are confident about everything, especially on their first attempt.

It is worth thinking about your confidence in the following areas:

- self-esteem;
- knowledge;
- communication;
- accepting support and help;
- self-acceptance.

The following SAQ is designed to get you thinking about your sources of self-confidence. Use it to boost your awareness of what you can do, even if you believe that 'pride comes before a fall' and that you should never boast.

4 Answer the questions under each of the following headings to explore your self-confidence. Where there are boxes for you to tick, choose just one box in each case.

Self-esteem

1 Can you tell a friend or relative when you have done something well? (This doesn't mean to Olympic standard, just better than usual.)

Yes ☐   No ☐   Sometimes ☐

2 Spend five minutes making a list of the main things you have achieved in your life. (Use a fresh sheet of paper if you prefer.)

Now look at your list.

3 Were you stuck about what to put on your list?

Yes ☐   No ☐

4 Did you let yourself make a long list with lots of different sorts of items on it?

Yes ☐   No ☐

For example:

Getting my Counselling Diploma
Having and bringing up the children
Caring for Uncle Alan
Influencing the outcome of the bypass enquiry
Landscaping the garden

5 Ask one or two good friends what they think you do well. Do you agree with them, and why, or why not?

6 If you do not agree, are your own standards for yourself unrealistic or harsh? (Many people are tougher on themselves than they are on others. Consider whether this applies to you.)

(continued overleaf)

Knowledge

1 Do you feel optimistic that you can grasp the facts of a situation?

Yes ☐   No ☐   Sometimes ☐

2 Are you good at drawing a general point from a series of details?

Yes ☐   No ☐   Sometimes ☐

3 Can you remember what you need to, and when you need to?

Yes ☐   No ☐   Sometimes ☐

4 How do you remember detailed information?

For example:

I learned the sequence of the Kings and Queens of England as a schoolgirl by a rhyme based on their first names.

5 How do you recall key ideas? Is it different from the way you remember detailed information?

For example:

I had to develop my own definitions of key words in Sociology before I felt confident in using the ideas.

Communication

1 Do you usually understand what others are saying to you?

Yes ☐   No ☐   Sometimes ☐

2 Do you often feel lost but unable to ask for an explanation?

Yes ☐   No ☐   Sometimes ☐

(continued opposite)

3   Do you ask tutors to define a word which is new to you?

Yes ☐   No ☐   Sometimes ☐

4   Do others usually understand you?

Yes ☐   No ☐   Sometimes ☐

5   Are you often asked to repeat yourself or explain your meaning?

Yes ☐   No ☐   Sometimes ☐

6   Are you most confident and effective when you are talking or when you are writing? (In other words, which do you choose to use when you have something complicated to explain?)

Accepting support and help

It is not easy to complete a course without some encouragement and support.

1   Can you ask others to put themselves out for you, for example, by making you supper while you study?

Yes ☐   No ☐   Sometimes ☐

2   Who can you ask for help and what can you ask them to do?

Person who can help: **by:**

Self-acceptance

It is important to know how to set yourself realistic and achievable goals.

1   Can you settle for what you can do, even when it is not all you might, or would ideally want to?

Yes ☐   No ☐   Sometimes ☐

2   Are you tolerant and accepting of your own limits when you make a mistake?

Yes ☐   No ☐   Sometimes ☐

Now review your responses to this SAQ and consider:

■ whether each of the factors (self-esteem, knowledge, and so on) affects your self-confidence about being assessed;

■ which factor is a source of confidence for you, and which is an area where your self-confidence is less well established;

■ whether the requirements of your course are a good match with your established strengths as identified by your notes;

■ whether you have more confidence in your flexibility to adapt to different needs or more confidence in your capacity to plan ahead and stick to a plan. (Which of these elements is strongest in your notes?);

■ what you need to develop further in order to do yourself more justice in your next assessment.

Write any comments below:

Developing confidence

You will need to develop a strategy for tackling the aspects of assessment you are most unsure of. Many people working towards assessment identify similar areas that they need to consider. This workbook aims to help in some of these key areas:

■ planning: including setting realistic goals and meeting deadlines – **Unit 5**;

■ benefiting from your tutor's comments during your course (formative assessment) – **Unit 6**;

■ preparing for assessment of essays, projects, portfolios, and journals – **Unit 7**;

■ how to adjust to assessment if you are a perfectionist – **Unit 8**;

■ how to control anxiety – **Unit 9**;

■ how to revise effectively and techniques for revision – **Units 10** and **11**;

■ answering the question – for essays, whether in exams or not – **Unit 12**;

■ getting it right on the day – for both assessments in general and exams in particular – **Unit 13**.

You may like to concentrate on those units you feel will help you develop your confidence.

Summary

This unit has helped you review what motivates you in your learning, how you feel about assessment, your sources of self-confidence and aspects of your assessment process which you need to work on to build your self-confidence.

In the next unit I will look at a key aspect for many in improving self-confidence: being thoroughly prepared by planning for the assessment.

UNIT 5

PLANNING FOR ASSESSMENT

What this unit is about

This unit looks at ways of ensuring that you take a planned approach to assessment, based on a clear understanding of the critical deadlines involved.

By the time you finish your work on this unit you should be able to:

→   state your attitude to deadlines;

→   describe your assessment deadlines;

→   plan how to do a piece of work;

→   set yourself SMART goals.

Are deadlines your friends or your enemies?

Whatever the form of your assessment it is likely either to take place on a specified day, or to need to be submitted by a certain date. In this way deadlines form a part of the assessment process and it is essential to be aware of your attitude to them and to plan your work accordingly.

Some students find deadlines very helpful in drawing up a plan to submit work. Others feel increasingly frozen as a deadline approaches, and do better when they can choose within quite a broad period when they will submit work.

1 Consider your own attitude to deadlines by thinking about the last deadline you had to meet. It could be related to work or your studies or even your home life.

1   In what ways was the deadline helpful to you?

2   In what ways, if any, did the deadline inhibit you, or prevent you from doing your best?

My experience of working to a deadline on this book is that it increased my anxiety that I would not produce work of a good enough standard, but that it was very successful in making this work a higher priority than other demands on my time. I think this is a common experience.

Getting the balance of anxiety right is more than just a matter of luck. You need to learn how much pressure is useful to help you get down to what needs to be done, and how to be accepting of your own limits when the pressure is making you unproductive.

Some people feel they have a clear direction if they have frequent deadlines to meet. Other people are overwhelmed by frequent deadlines and feel that they get in the way of any broader learning.

Each person has their own pattern, and capitalising on your own will make you more effective and less stressed.

It is helpful to review your aims in learning and to set yourself achievable goals. In particular, systematic planning to meet your assessment commitments allows you to do the important tasks, rather than always being driven by the urgent ones.

Before you look at how to plan, it is worth thinking further about the deadlines you need to meet.

Your assessment deadlines

In Unit 2 I asked you to draw up a chart showing your assessment structure. This should show you the kinds of deadlines you have to meet and their frequency. For example, in some courses students have to submit essays or assignments. They may also have assessment days throughout the year, when students have to demonstrate a skill to an assessor. In other courses the deadlines are centred around end-of-course exams, though tutors set deadlines for submission of coursework.

2 Consider the pattern of deadlines in your course by reviewing your work in Unit 2, if appropriate, and answering the following questions. You may not know precise deadlines at this stage, but be as specific as possible.

1   What deadlines do you have for formative assessments (these are assessments that do not count towards your final grade or qualification)?

2   What deadlines do you have for summative assessments (these are assessments that do count towards your final grade or qualification)?

3   Which of these deadlines are unmovable – in other words, you have to meet them or incur penalties – and which ones are negotiable? Tick the unmovable ones and put a question mark next to those you may be able to negotiate.

Exam dates and days when you are going to be observed by an assessor will tend to be rigidly set, with no room for manoeuvre.

Dates for submitting essays, assignments, portfolios and journals for summative assessment are also likely to be set, although there may be one or two days of leeway.

You should find out what leeway you have and, if there is a penalty for late submission, what it is. Some courses reduce a student's essay or project grade by ten per cent for each day late. Students may decide to put a piece of work in a day late because they believe they can still improve their grade over the penalty, but this can be risky.

There is likely to be more scope to negotiate deadlines for formative assessment work. You may be able to agree deadlines with your tutor so that they fit into your schedule.

When you are in charge of setting your own deadlines you should set a realistic one so you can be satisfied with the quality of your work, but still meet your other obligations. It can be helpful to discuss such deadlines with your tutor or a friend, or those at home, to check whether you can meet them.

Whatever your deadlines are, you need to be clear about rules for exceptional circumstances. For example, if you are ill or have a crisis, does the system permit extensions? Do you need a doctor's certificate?

Assessment deadlines do not go away, and it is important to be prepared for them. This means careful planning.

Planning

Undertaking assessable courses or work-based S/NVQ assessments requires preparation. Any assessment has a performance element and, like the old troupers of the theatre or athletes who are running a marathon, you need to be willing to prepare actively for the event.

To prepare, you need to decide what action to take. This will depend on the type of assessment.

For example, if you have to give a presentation to an audience on a certain day, you may decide that you need to do the following:

- find out what aspects of the presentation will be assessed (by reading the syllabus, assessment criteria or similar documents);

- make sure you know enough about the subject you will be talking about;

- find out who your audience is so you can pitch your presentation at the right level to suit it;

- plan what points you want to make in the time you have to give the presentation;

- decide which audio-visual aids will help get your points across and ensure that the equipment – such as a slide projector – will be available;

- summarise your presentation in easy-to-read note form;

- practise giving the presentation, so you can test for the time it takes and whether it runs smoothly, and amend your approach if necessary;

- do a practice presentation in front of some friends, so that you identify the things you feel confident of conveying. Invite their suggestions for improvements and be prepared to run through it again.

With a list of tasks like this, you can begin to plan how to fit each one into your schedule, so that you will be well prepared for the assessment.

Sketching a broad timetable is useful because it helps you to allocate a reasonable time for each task. For instance, in the list of tasks for the presentation, you would want to set aside more time for planning the points you want to make than for finding out about your audience. But it is sensible to keep a close eye on any timetable or plan to make sure that it is realistic and that you can implement it. At an early stage it is essential to review the plan to see if you are keeping to it. If not, you will need to revise your plan, or make changes in your other commitments so you can still carry out all the tasks you set yourself.

When you come to carry out each task you need to do more planning. This involves setting explicit goals that are SMART:

- **S**pecific;
- **M**easurable;
- **A**ppropriate/adequate;
- **R**ealistic;
- **T**ime limited.

Let's look at each of these in more detail:

Specific

You should describe precisely what you want to do. For example, if you say before you start: 'I will do two hours' work tonight' you may spend two hours doing nothing useful. It is better to be specific about what you want to achieve, for example, 'Tonight I will plan the first assignment and identify my gaps in information ready for library time tomorrow.'

Measurable

It is useful to be able to check that you have done what you set out to do. If you say, 'I will read Chapter 2 as part of my essay preparation', a day later you may not remember what you learned in that chapter, and may even wonder whether you did read it. It is more sensible to say, 'I will read Chapter 2 and make notes of the information that is relevant for my essay.' This way you will have a record of your work and a basis for testing your recall of the material.

Appropriate/adequate

You may set a goal that is specific and measurable, but unless you have thought about whether or not it is sufficient it may not be an adequate goal. For example, you may set aside one evening to write an essay from scratch, but this may not be enough time to do the job properly.

On the other hand, you must aim to do no more than is sufficient to do the job properly. Otherwise you may overload yourself with work, and then feel so daunted that you do not get around to doing any of it.

For any goal you set it is worth considering whether what you plan to do will be appropriate and adequate to cover what is required.

Realistic

It is demoralising if you set yourself a goal that is impossible to achieve in the time you have available. If you are planning to work for two hours, you should ask yourself what you can reasonably expect to achieve in that time. You should aim to achieve a sensible amount for the time and energy you have available.

Time limited

Every goal can usefully have a time limit attached to focus your energies and to allow you to review whether or not you have achieved it.

One of the tasks listed on page 33 for preparing for a presentation was:

> find out what aspects of the presentation will be assessed (by reading the syllabus, assessment criteria or similar document).

Write this out as a SMART goal:

Here is my suggestion:

Read the part of the syllabus on presentation skills and list everything the assessor will be looking for when I give my presentation. Spend half an hour on this.

Your suggestion is likely to be different from mine, but it should be specific, measurable, adequate, realistic and time limited.

You can apply these SMART criteria to any aspect of setting goals and planning.

Plan the next piece of work you need to do. Use separate sheets of paper and your diary or calendar, and use the following steps as a guide.

1   Note down the deadline for the work.
2   Decide what you need to do to complete the work.
3   Make a list of everything you need to do.
4   Write out a timetable, allocating time for each task. Remember to allow time for your other commitments, as well.
5   Check your timetable, perhaps with the help of a close friend to make sure you have been realistic in your planning.
6   Set yourself SMART goals for the tasks before you have to do them.
7   Carry out your plan, but remember to check whether you are keeping to your timetable, and amend it as necessary.

There is no such thing as a perfect plan, as circumstances are bound to change when you carry it out. But if you keep track of where you are in your plan and take steps to modify it if you fall behind, you should be able to stay on target and meet your deadlines.

Summary

In this unit you have considered how you feel about deadlines and looked at the kind of assessment deadlines you will need to meet. Systematic preparation to meet any deadline is essential, and the key to this is careful planning. You have been introduced to ways of setting SMART goals and to planning a piece of work.

UNIT 6 USING COURSEWORK EFFECTIVELY

What this unit is about

In your course you are likely to do a number of formative assessments. These do not count towards your final qualification. Instead the aim is to help you to learn and develop. So a key aspect of formative assessments is learning from the comments and suggestions made by the person or people doing the assessing.

By the time you have completed your work on this unit you should be able to:

→   get the most out of comments on your work;

→   ask your tutor to make comments and suggestions that will help you with your assessment.

Who assesses you?

In formative assessments such as essays, assignments or demonstrations, the person assessing you is most likely to be your tutor. But depending on your circumstances you may have other people, such as a boss or fellow students or colleagues, who act as assessors.

If your assessment is in the form of a computer generated test or quiz or multiple-choice questions, a computer may 'mark' your work and send you feedback.

Making use of comments

It is seldom easy to receive critical comments, however helpfully they are intended. When someone else with more knowledge or a different perspective makes suggestions about work that you have struggled to produce, you need a lot of self-confidence to accept that it is your product which is being improved, and that you personally are not being attacked.

To benefit from comments, you need to trust that the person assessing your work has good intentions towards you.

Generally your tutor is an ally, and is interested in helping you develop. Part of the tutor's role is to identify your developmental needs and direct his or her comments on your formative assessments accordingly. Your tutor should help you to identify whether you are on the right lines in any piece of work (written, practical or oral) and if not, what you need to do differently.

However, you also have a role to play in assessing your work. This role can be split into two:

1 spending time thinking about how you rate your work;

2 giving your tutor feedback on how helpful you find his or her comments.

If you are familiar with the syllabus and assessment requirements (see Unit 3) you may be well suited to judge the areas where you are strong and where you need help.

1 Think about the skills, knowledge and attitudes you need to develop in your course. Note down two from these areas that you feel confident about, and one or two that you feel less sure of (you may find it helpful to refer back to SAQ 1 in Unit 3):

Assessment requirements I feel confident I can meet:

Assessment requirements I feel unsure about being able to meet:

You may like to talk to your tutor about your assessment; can you ask for comments on these aspects?

One aspect of formative assessment that you may be able to negotiate with your tutor is deadlines. Just as your tutor may expect work to be handed in by a certain time, you should be able to expect feedback on your work by a certain time. There is little benefit from guidance offered after you have moved on to the next part of the work. Prompt feedback is more encouraging and supportive.

If comments on a piece of work do not match your expectations, you should seek to find out why. It is worth telling your tutor the kind of comments you were expecting. This can sometimes help to clarify any problems and misunderstandings.

Similarly, if you disagree with the comments or simply do not understand the point of them it is usually possible to ask for more detail on or explanation of a particular suggestion or point.

Make sure that you are clear about how the work you have submitted would be assessed if it were part of your summative assessment.

For example, if your course is based on criterion referenced assessment, your tutor should relate your work to the standards you are aiming to meet, and show which aspects of your work meet the standards, which aspects do not meet specific standards, and which areas need improvement.

You need to feel comfortable with the feedback you receive. If this is not the case, and if you do not trust that the person assessing you is an ally, you are unlikely to benefit from the comments. In such a case, see if you can get informal comments from someone well qualified whom you do trust. If you can, you will be much more likely to act on those and learn from them.

2 This SAQ will help you consider your attitude to feedback from assessment. Answer the following questions about your course or programme of study.

Whose opinion do you seek on your progress?

What comments about your work have you found helpful in the last few months?

Why were they helpful?

What comments have been unhelpful?

Why were they unhelpful? (Because of the way they were given, or because of your feelings about the person who gave them, or because it was uncomfortable to get critical comments?)

What will you need to do to get the best out of any comments which may come your way on your course?

Is there someone whose advice you will seek in the next few weeks?

Formative assessment should help develop your confidence in your ability to go forward for a qualification. It is essential to seek early and frequent comments about what you are getting right as well as what you need to do better. When assessments do not count towards your final course grade they give you a valuable opportunity to develop your understanding of what is expected of you, without putting your achievement of the qualification at risk.

If your course does not offer much direct formative assessment from a tutor or similar person, you may like to team up with another student to:

■ discuss aspects of the course;

■ test each other;

■ offer mutual encouragement.

Computer marked assessments

Good computer programs will do more than tell you your score; they will tell you which questions you answered wrongly, asterisk sections on which you earned high or low scores, and even retain a record of your score from one attempt to the next, so that you can measure your improvement.

So if your course offers you the opportunity to use computer marked assessments, it is worth taking advantage of the opportunity. If you are in charge of deciding when to take them, monitor your learning so you take them when you can get most out of them: that is, when you are fairly sure you have grasped the main ideas.

Learning from multiple-choice quizzes

If your course involves multiple-choice assessment, you need to know the scoring system. In particular, you need to know whether you are given points for each right answer, and whether you have points deducted for each wrong answer.

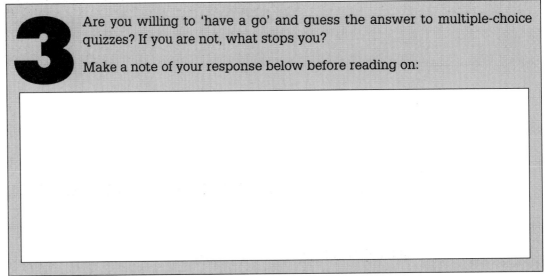

Are you willing to 'have a go' and guess the answer to multiple-choice quizzes? If you are not, what stops you?

Make a note of your response below before reading on:

A good test should be constructed with more than a simple yes/no or true/false option, so you are being tested on what you know, not on a 50–50 chance of guessing. Each wrong answer (known as a 'distracter') is there because it reveals particular misunderstandings. So even if you do not immediately and confidently know the right answer, you may find you can work it out by thinking about it in general terms first.

Getting feedback when you start an assessment

Many courses involve some continuous summative assessment, such as essays completed during a course whose assessment goes towards the final grade or qualification. If this is the case for you, it is worth asking for formative assessment at the planning stages of the product (whether it is an essay, assignment, portfolio, or something you are making).

Your tutor knows you personally and may be just as interested in how you are approaching the task as in the final product. The aim of such formative assessment is to give you clear, specific, positive criticism and encouragement so you can do yourself justice in the piece of work.

For instance, a formative assessment about an essay you are writing might enable you to clarify and discuss some of the following points while the work is in progress:

- What is the purpose of this piece of writing?

- Who is it aimed at?

- Is the audience addressed in appropriate language?

- Have you understood what the question is about?

- Have you shown what you know in answer to the question?

- What other information would be relevant? Do you know where to look for it?

- Is your presentation logical? Clear? Persuasive?

You can use this formative assessment to improve your essay before it is presented for summative assessment.

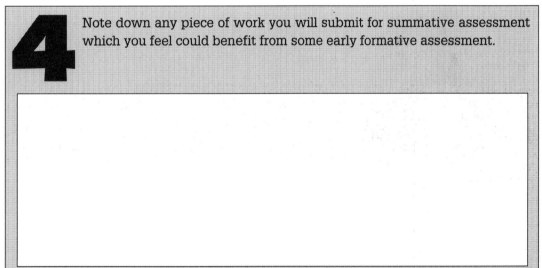

Note down any piece of work you will submit for summative assessment which you feel could benefit from some early formative assessment.

Summary

In this unit you have considered how to get the most from comments you receive as part of your work on the course.

In the next unit you will look at work that is normally completed during the course and submitted for summative assessment.

UNIT 7

ESSAYS, PROJECTS, PORTFOLIOS AND JOURNALS

What this unit is about

This unit looks at some of the main ways, other than formal exams, in which you can provide a demonstration of your knowledge or skills. It suggests how you can tackle these in a way that maximises your chances of success. This involves looking at forms of assessment that – apart from essays – may be unfamiliar to you. All offer potentially exciting opportunities to demonstrate your knowledge and skill, and put the initiative for assessment more firmly on you, the student, than more traditional forms of testing.

By the time you finish your work on this unit you should be able to:

→   list what you need to clarify before starting work on:

an essay;

a project;

a portfolio;

a journal.

→   state the key points you need to bear in mind when writing essays, projects, portfolios and journals.

Initial planning

I'll begin this unit by looking at what is common to all these types of work. I'll then go on to consider some of the points you need to bear in mind when tackling each of the four specific forms of assessment. First, though, let me make it clear what I am talking about.

■   By **essay** I mean a single piece of written work up to about 2000 words long, generally completed in a fortnight or less.

■   By **project** I mean a more substantial piece of written work, completed over a longer period – anything from six to eight weeks to six months. You may sometimes find a project referred to as an 'extended essay'.

■   By **portfolio** I mean a set of often varied materials arranged around a particular topic or theme. Again, this is usually completed over an extended period.

■   By **journal** I mean – well, a journal! But in the context of assessment this is likely to be linked to a particular topic or activity, rather than be a general record of your daily life.

You may also come across the term 'assignment'. This is frequently used in relation to NVQs and SVQs, and usually refers to a short project – which in some cases may be nothing more than an essay.

Now we've considered the terminology, let's turn to another point of clarification: your own brief.

Clarifying your brief

When approaching any of these types of work you can expect from your tutor a brief explanation of what you should do. Specific words in your brief will tell you not just what you are expected to know, eg:

> *The student should be able to name six cabinet members.*

but also the assessment criteria – how you will be judged as knowing them, eg:

> *The student should be able to spell their names correctly, and connect them to the right Departments of State.*

Before you embark on your work you will also need to check:

- how long it is expected to be;
- what resources you can draw on.

 Use the following checklist to clarify key issues before you start work:

Length

- Are there any limits on words or number of items presented? If so, what are they?
- If there are word limits, what is their purpose? Are they:
    - to encourage you to set yourself realistic and limited goals?
    - to help you to practise being concise and focused?
    - to limit the work of the tutors who have to mark your material?
- What penalties are incurred if you go over the limits?
- What can you do if you are significantly under the limit but cannot think of anything to add? Can you:
    - check the task?
    - check the reading list?
    - ask your tutor or other students for guidance?

Resources

- Have you made preliminary notes on the topic(s) you want to cover, to guide your search for resources?
- Have you checked that the resources you need are readily available (eg by contacting your library or resource centre)?
- Have you identified a second choice of topic in case the resources you need for your first choice cannot be obtained?

Setting yourself goals

The longer your piece of work, the more helpful it is to set yourself a series of goals. Each of these goals should have a deadline attached to help ensure that work does not pile up at the end – though you should be prepared to review and revise these deadlines as your work proceeds. Check that each goal is SMART – see page 34.

Here are some basic guidelines for researching and presenting your work. You can treat each one as a goal to work towards. These notes apply to all the forms of work discussed in this unit, except journals:

- Review the question or topic until you have analysed it from all angles and you feel confident you understand what is wanted of you, and what the criteria are for assessment. If published criteria are available, check what these are (you may need your tutor's help to interpret them).

- Start to collect your material and organise it so you can find it easily. Use a library or resource centre, and use contents pages or indexes to ensure you are consulting key sources.

- Look out for any structure which is emerging as you continue to make notes or gather material. As soon as this structure suggests itself, begin to organise your findings into sections that match it.

- Book a session with your tutor and/or other students to review your progress and ensure that your work is on the right lines. Check that your material is still relevant to your theme and follows the criteria for assessment.

- Prepare your first draft. Use visual material where possible to save words and make your point more clearly.

- If possible, leave your completed draft for a few days, so that you can look over your material with a fresh eye. If there is not time to do this, ask someone you trust to review it and give you their reactions. Check particularly that you have stayed within your brief.

- Prepare your final draft.

- Deliver your material to your tutor. If you have to mail it, keep a copy if you can: work has been known to get lost in the post.

Working with others

Whatever sort of assessment you are preparing for, it can be useful to discuss your approach with other students, and even agree what material is relevant. Provided you do not copy someone else's work in detail, which is of course unacceptable, your presentation will be your unique synthesis, yet you will have had the advantage of comparing your ideas with those of other students.

2 Now identify which of the four types of assessment described in this unit you will need to tackle. If your course involves several, choose the one with which you feel you need most help. Then note down your answers to the following questions:

- On what topics will you be assessed?

(continued overleaf)

■ How extensive should your work be (eg word limits, number of items in a portfolio)?

■ When does the work need to be completed by?

■ What resources will you need access to?

■ Who could you discuss your plans with?

You may now want to focus on the sections below that deal with your particular form of assessment. However, I suggest you at least skim through the whole unit, since many of the comments I make about specific sorts of assessment usually apply to some extent to the others as well.

Answering essay questions

At A level and beyond, essay questions often invite a case to be made for or against a specific assertion. The assessor will expect you to back up your opinion with a reasoned argument. You will also gain marks for balance. Your aim should be to examine the evidence for both sides of your case, and then justify your support for one side or the other. This reviewing of evidence to create an argument, rather than a simple agreement or disagreement, is a key skill which is being tested. A wishy-washy conclusion which simply says there are points to be made on both sides will not get you many marks.

Bear in mind, too, that you will gain marks by writing convincingly about a debate, not by providing a startling new analysis which the assessor as expert in the field has never considered. Your assessor will be working to a marking scheme which will give marks for:

- relevant information;

- the organisation of your argument;

- the validity of the conclusion you are drawing from your evidence.

Approaching an essay question

There are two main approaches to answering an essay question, the 'jury' and the 'advocate' methods. Both involve writing out your answer in a logical sequence, but the nature of the sequence differs in each case.

The 'jury' method

This proceeds as follows:

- Begin with definitions of key terms, as you will be using them.

- Put forward the evidence on both sides of the argument.

- End (in your concluding paragraph) with the verdict.

Remember that your verdict is very unlikely to be a simple opinion. Your task is most commonly to weigh up the evidence for and against, and then offer a considered judgement.

The 'advocate' method

Here the procedure is as follows:

- Put your verdict in your first paragraph.

- Give your definitions of key terms.

- Build the rest of your essay to support your verdict.

The advocate approach has the advantage of signposting to the busy assessor what view you will be supporting and how strongly. You will be marshalling your evidence both for and against your view in the same way as in a jury essay.

In either approach your final verdict may be that there is a lot of truth in the statement, or very little. It is worth choosing one of these rather than suggesting that the arguments are evenly balanced, since sitting on the fence is not a convincing way of being persuasive – which is what is being tested!

At the end of your essay you may usefully relate the topic to other significant issues. If you can put the subject into perspective in this way you will finish with some impact, rather than a bland summary of your position.

Two tips for answering essay questions

- If on reading through your essay it seems to be just a long list of facts, you may have missed the point (unless of course your key verb was 'describe'). Check the verb again and see if you can add a final paragraph to show the relevance of the facts to your verdict. (There is more about key verbs on pages 81–2.)

- If you are writing your essay in an exam, don't waste time writing out the question at the top of your answer, or repeating it in your first sentence. If you write down the question number that will be sufficient for the examiner to identify it.

3 Carry out this SAQ if you selected essays as your priority topic in SAQ 1.

Consider your initial plans for your essay. Make a note below of:

■ your topic:

■ the key verb:

■ the method you will try – jury or advocate;

■ your timetable:

    – for completing your full plan:

    – for submitting your finished essay:

Projects

Many students find projects particularly satisfying, because they provide the opportunity to do an extended piece of work more in tune with their own particular interests and priorities. They also welcome the chance to present their work in more varied ways than simply writing, or the opportunity to carry out direct research.

As with essays, you will need to ensure that your work is structured in a way that makes your purpose crystal clear to your assessor. And as with essays, you will need to work to a clear set of goals. However, projects present more of a challenge to assessors because of the variety of possible approaches to the task. For this reason you can expect to be provided with a very clear specification of what is required. In fact, if you feel in the least unclear about assessment requirements don't hesitate to check with your tutor before your work gets under way. Your specification should include details of:

■ how much work you are expected to present;

■ the theme or topic of your project;

■ any specific sources you are expected to consult (eg. a particular directory or report);

■ how you should present your work.

The last point is important. Bear in mind that what matters in the end is the content of your project. You will not gain additional marks for going beyond the presentation specified, eg with expensive bindings or fancy pictures! You may, however, be expected to show evidence of skills with a wordprocessor or database. Check with your tutor and course regulations for guidance on this and other aspects of presentation.

Your aim in any project work should be to communicate what you know, understand and can do. As with all writing, it is important to be aware of your audience. Ask yourself: 'What does my reader need to make sense of my work?' Don't forget the value of practice and obtaining feedback on this. This applies whatever skills you are developing in your project: writing, drawing, making calculations, laying out your work so that it is inviting to read, or constructing your analysis.

4 Carry out this SAQ if you selected projects as your priority topic in SAQ 1.

Make your initial plans for your project. Make a note below of:

■ your topic:

■ people whose help you could draw on:

■ materials (eg books, reports) you will need:

■ your timetable:

   — for completing your plan:

   — for submitting your finished project:

Portfolios

Portfolios are frequently required on courses leading to an NVQ or GNVQ qualification. As I suggested on page 43, they are collections of a range of materials, compiled as evidence that an agreed set of criteria have been met. The work may have been carried out in the course of normal employment – paid or unpaid – and need not have originally been prepared for assessment purposes.

Items in a portfolio can include essays, projects, and assignments; but non-written material is also admissible, and frequently encouraged. For example, assessment of competence in communication skills could make use of an audio tape or video; a portfolio for a diploma in business skills could include samples of office reports and memos; a course in interior design could be assessed using scale models of rooms, as well as more traditional written work.

The key issues for students assembling portfolios are:

How much to include?

Check carefully what is required. It is usually better to err on the side of fewer items, all of which are directly relevant, rather than a larger number which demonstrate your competence less clearly.

What format should you use?

For example, if you have to include a transcript of a tape showing your skill in a meeting, group or interview, are you expected to supply written notes with it to make clear why you were present and what your aims were? Or if you are including photographs, are you expected to explain why they were chosen, or how they were taken?

How should work be presented?

Most portfolios consist of a loose collection of material. This presents a challenge not present in other forms of assessment. How will you ensure that this is kept together, and in the right sequence? Do you need a looseleaf file? A folder? A box? As in the case of projects, you should check with your tutor and course regulations to help you in your decision.

How recent should items be?

Usually each item needs to be dated to show that you have completed it during a specified period. You will need to check whether there are any dates of production before which material is regarded as too old to be allowed as evidence of competence.

5 Carry out this SAQ if you selected portfolios as your priority topic in SAQ 1.

Make your initial plans for your portfolio. Make a note below of:

■ the sorts of item you intend to include in your portfolio:

(continued opposite)

■ any points you need to bear in mind about format:

■ what presentation you will select – eg ringbinder, folder, box;

■ your timetable:

– for completing your plan:

– for submitting your finished portfolio:

Journals

Many personal development courses require students to keep journals. These are usually one form of assessment among others, rather than the sole means. Journals are designed to be a personal record of things such as thoughts, feelings, reactions to experiential learning, application of ideas to work or life outside the course. They can be used:

■ as part of an overall portfolio;

■ to record points you wish to bring up at tutorial sessions or in discussion with other students;

■ as briefing for others (eg your tutor) before a tutorial;

■ to demonstrate how you are applying course ideas to your workplace.

Their advantage is that they enable you to compile an ongoing record of your personal development, broken down into manageable chunks of writing. They are a particularly useful way of recording what you have learned. Indeed, they can be used as evidence of achievement even when a project or assignment ends in apparent failure – provided that you are able to show what you learned from this.

Students are usually told at the start what topics they should be addressing in their journal, but the form of writing is not usually specified. Some journals are structured so that there is description on one page and analysis on a facing page. So, for example, you could on opposite pages:

■ record what happened when you attempted to put a new skill into practice (eg summarising during a meeting);

■ analyse the experience in terms of:

– your intention;

– your feelings about trying it;

– your assessment of the effectiveness of your summary.

6 Carry out this SAQ if you selected journals as your priority topic in SAQ 1.

Make your initial plans for your journal. Make a note below of:

■ your topic:

■ what you will use to write your entries in:

■ who you are writing for: your eyes only – or someone else's? (It's important to be clear from the outset how confidential – or legible – your entries are going to be.):

■ how often you will write entries. (Regularity may be less important than frequency.):

■ your timetable:

– for beginning your journal:

– for submitting your finished journal:

Summary

In this unit we have looked at a range of ways of demonstrating your skill or knowledge. Most of these have involved written work. I have encouraged you to take a planned approach, with a schedule that takes account of initial preparation as well as intermediate and final deadlines. In all work of this sort it is vital to aim as high as possible. But it is also important not to set yourself impossible targets. This last point is so important that I am devoting the whole of the next unit to it.

UNIT

8

COPING WITH PERFECTIONISM

What this unit is about

This unit looks at an approach to assessment that can be either a help or a hindrance: perfectionism. It helps you identify your own attitude to getting things right and suggests how to avoid excessive perfectionism.

By the time you finish your work on this unit you should be able to:

→ say whether or not you are a perfectionist;

→ describe how being a perfectionist affects performance in assessments, particularly exams;

→ plan how to adapt – if you are a perfectionist.

Are you a perfectionist?

Perfectionists want to get things right. Try this short SAQ to see if you are a perfectionist.

1   Look at these comments from students and tick those that you agree with or feel you might make at one time or another.

Tick:

1   *I love making myself a detailed timetable for revision, and get a kick out of sticking to it and crossing each item off.*   ☐

2   *I revise very thoroughly.*   ☐

3   *I make a resolution to write something every day and just get on with it.*   ☐

4   *I always feel I could do better.*   ☐

5   *The examiner will see how stupid I really am, and I feel so embarrassed that I can't do myself justice in an exam the way I do with lots of time for an assignment.*   ☐

6   *I hate not being able to do my best. I want to do well and when time's limited I won't be able to do the job as I would like to.*   ☐

7   *I hate the thought of getting less than a distinction.*   ☐

If you can identify with any of these comments then you are likely to be something of a perfectionist.

If you haven't ticked any of these comments, then you may see yourself as not perfectionist enough. You may even be at the other extreme and instead of 'trying hard' may actually be quite casual in your approach to assessment. This can be a big disadvantage.

If you have always been able to get by and do well with very little effort, it can be a problem to develop the discipline to study something which is more of a challenge. If you don't develop some systematic 'plodding' work habits, you may simply avoid those subjects that don't come easily. This is a matter of motivation. If you want to get a particular qualification you will need to find work habits which are good enough to get results. Just hoping for the best may let you down. You may find it helpful to refer back to Unit 5: 'Planning for Assessment'.

The rest of this unit aims to help people who are perfectionists.

Every personal style of studying has advantages and disadvantages, and perfectionism is no exception. If you are a perfectionist your strength is your commitment to getting your work right, and this is usually a potent engine for careful preparation and systematic planning. But perfectionists may set themselves unrealistically hard schedules, or have very self-critical inner voices.

Many perfectionists are still reacting to some significant person in their youth who said, in one way or another, 'You could do better.' Perfectionist students have spoken of parents who only ever remarked on the critical comments on their school reports, teachers who criticised or humiliated them in front of classmates, and so on.

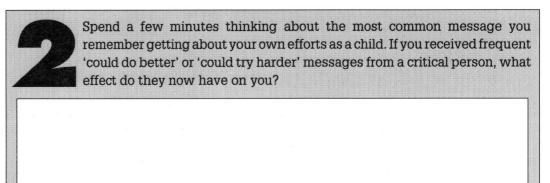

2 Spend a few minutes thinking about the most common message you remember getting about your own efforts as a child. If you received frequent 'could do better' or 'could try harder' messages from a critical person, what effect do they now have on you?

As a perfectionist myself, I know I was left believing I was very lazy. As an adult I often drive myself much too hard. For example, if I am unwell, I am inclined to think I am 'just slacking' unless I have real evidence of illness, such as a temperature. For study and exam purposes, this means I can push myself beyond the point of efficient study because I've given myself an unrealistic target and won't let go of it.

It may help you to identify YOUR critical person and establish that you are now studying to meet your own needs, and don't have to prove anything to him or her (though of course this is easier said than done).

Perfectionists in assessment

If you are a perfectionist you are likely to get good grades in your coursework and on any summative assessment you do during the course (continuous assessment). This is often because of the time and effort you are prepared to put in.

But it is worth considering whether other aspects of your work and personal life suffer unduly as a result of such intensive work. If you feel it does perhaps you can think about how to amend your approach.

Consider the '80/20 rule'. This states that in a huge variety of circumstances, you get a piece of work about 80 per cent right in the first 20 per cent of effort you spend. Think about it! If all you need to do is to get your answer 80 per cent right, it may be more feasible to let go of the wish to produce something 100 per cent right, and settle for getting on with the 80 per cent that could be comfortably within your grasp. The benefit lies in letting go of the critical inner voice saying 'You should be doing better than this!'

You also need to schedule for time off from working on assessments for relaxation, recreation and refreshment. Working all the time makes you stale and inefficient. It is much better to take a break and come back to your work with fresh enthusiasm.

3 If you are a perfectionist tackling continuous assessment, what action can you take to make sure that you get the work done and also meet your other commitments – both to other people and to yourself?

You may find that the key is in realistic planning. See Unit 5 to check whether the goals you set yourself are SMART.

Perfectionists in exams

Exams are more difficult for perfectionists to cope with, because exams have a set time limit. If you are a perfectionist you need to understand the different nature of the exam process and be willing to adapt your approach to it.

You need to do your preparatory thinking before the exam to counteract any habit of prolonged thinking around a topic before beginning to put pen to paper. Units 10, 11 and 12 should help you prepare. You may also find it helpful to think of the 80/20 rule, described above.

4 The following are perfectionists' most frequently cited fears about exams. Tick those which bother you, and note whether you feel they are minor concerns or significant worries which you'd like to discuss with a good listener or fellow students:

Tick:

I'm too slow to do myself justice in an exam. ☐

My memory will let me down. I'll forget key points. ☐

I'll be caught out and shown up as a fraud who doesn't REALLY know what I pretend to. ☐

I haven't done enough work to deserve to pass. ☐

Unless I've read everything and remembered it all I shall be caught out. ☐

Unless I've understood everything it's not worth taking the exam. ☐

Now look at the following comments, which are designed to help you reconsider how far these fears are based in truth:

Slowness of thinking or writing

Slow thinking needs to be tackled at the revision stage. (See Unit 10)

Slow writing is a difficulty. If you have any physical disability which affects the speed at which you can write you need to inform the exam board at the time of registration and they may make special arrangements for you. If not, PRACTISE until you are writing more quickly, aiming for somewhere between 500 and 700 words for a 40-minute essay answer, yet still with reasonable legibility. Examiners rarely penalise poor handwriting.

It is worth remembering that it is quality of argument that counts more than quantity of words. It is more important to have learned and practised ways to plan an answer quickly than to worry about slow writing.

Memory

Anxiety affects your memory. But revision practice about identifying and recalling essential information will help (see Unit 11). Your work in Unit 3 on making sure of what is required in your assessment is important too. Most exams test your capacity for arguing a case much more than they test straightforward memory.

Feeling a fraud

Few students realise that most examiners' marking schemes are designed to give marks for every point being made. The examiner is not generally trying to catch you out, but looking for ways to pass you. If you have had an opportunity to see the marking scheme you will have clearer ideas about what you are required to do to accumulate marks, but even if you have not seen it your preparatory revision to identify relevant points will help you to think about how to do so.

Knowing it all

Very few exams deduct marks for errors, yet a dislike of making mistakes often inhibits perfectionists from putting down points they have thought of but are not completely sure about.

If you feel you don't deserve to pass unless you've been a perfect student, you perhaps need to substitute a more reasonable and encouraging tone in your conversations with yourself! For example, instead of 'I don't deserve to pass' you might tell yourself: 'I have done some work, and it's worth doing my best now.' If you are stuck with being in the exam room you might as well be kind to yourself and have a go.

All students can benefit if they use the revision period to do a systematic and overall review of the course.

All real learning is characterised by some sense of 'not knowing' or 'not knowing enough'. But if you have passed your continuous assessment and/or got encouraging comments in formative assessment you should know and understand enough to tackle the exam after some focused revision. Exams cannot offer you an opportunity to demonstrate all you know; they are too brief a sample of work. But they can show how you construct an argument or respond to a previously unseen question about the material you have been studying.

5 Note down any action you – as a perfectionist – can now take to prepare for an exam.

Summary

This unit should have helped you prepare for assessment if you are a perfectionist. You have looked at the advantages and disadvantages of being a perfectionist and have planned some ways of overcoming the disadvantages.

The next unit looks at how to overcome excessive nervousness before assessment.

UNIT
9

MANAGING ANXIETY

What this unit is about

This unit looks at the feeling most commonly associated with assessment: anxiety. It shows how you can make anxiety work for you, as well as how to cope when the going gets tough.

By the time you finish your work on this unit you should be able to:

➜   explain how some anxiety can help in assessments;

➜   say whether you suffer from excess anxiety;

➜   practise some techniques to help you overcome nervousness.

Using anxiety

Most of your assessments involve you in being judged, and you probably want to do as well as you possibly can. When you have limited opportunities to show what you can do, some level of anxiety is not surprising.

Most people suffer some anxiety about assessment. It is not uncommon for people to report symptoms such as the following:

■   an occasional sleepless night;

■   waking early in the morning;

■   butterflies in the stomach just before the assessment;

■   reluctance to eat much breakfast on the day.

This level of pressure can work in your favour, enabling you to think efficiently and rapidly sift options, plan, recall relevant material, and so on.

If you have read about the experiences of any performer, you will probably know that they usually say it is the pressure of the task and the audience which helps them to turn in their outstanding performance.

Your assessment can be similar, and it is worth imagining your assessor or examiner as your audience – critical but ready to applaud your work.

But many people find anxiety about assessment overwhelming. For them the level of anxiety bears no direct relationship to their ability.

This is what one student said about submitting an assignment for assessment:

> When I put my assignment in to my tutor I panic, thinking I'll fail it, and I feel a minor form of what I feel in an exam: I'm not going to have done it right – no matter how hard I try it's going to be wrong – I can't possibly do it right – I don't care how much I know I'll still make mistakes. It's all my own stupid fault – and I feel very small and want to curl up very tiny – I'm certain I've done it wrong.

(She usually gets As and Bs!)

High levels of anxiety can adversely affect students in two ways:

- they may succeed in the end but suffer painfully in the process, and mind that others do not appreciate what it costs them;

- they may do significantly worse than their grades for coursework would lead them to expect.

Anxiety can be a problem in the preparation for assessment and – when the assessment involves some kind of performance, such as an interview, demonstration or exam – during the assessment itself.

It is important, then, to be aware of what causes you anxiety and to manage your anxiety levels so you can perform well.

Are you a worrier?

1 Consider your levels of anxiety by answering any of the following questions which are relevant to your circumstances. Tick the option that most nearly applies to you.

1 Do you tend to feel optimistic that 'It will all be all right on the day', and therefore do too little preparation for an assessment?

Always ☐   Sometimes ☐   Never ☐

2 Are you so relaxed in an assessment that you make errors of omission because of a lack of alertness?

Always ☐   Sometimes ☐   Never ☐

3 Are you at risk of missing deadlines because you just don't get around to starting work till too late?

Always ☐   Sometimes ☐   Never ☐

4 Do you do particularly badly in significant assessments, and better in ones that do not count?

Always ☐   Sometimes ☐   Never ☐

(continued opposite)

5   Do worry and tension affect your capacity to revise and remember, or prepare?

   Always ☐   Sometimes ☐   Never ☐

6   If you feel watched do you freeze up?

   Always ☐   Sometimes ☐   Never ☐

7   If you do badly, do you believe it indicates your lack of ability and/or of effort?

   Always ☐   Sometimes ☐   Never ☐

8   Do you go over and over assessments looking for what you may have got wrong?

   Always ☐   Sometimes ☐   Never ☐

9   Have you had a bad experience in an exam so that now you are anxious about assessments even though you are not generally anxious?

   Always ☐   Sometimes ☐   Never ☐

In general, students may fall into one of three different groups, each group needing a separate strategy to manage anxiety. These groups are as follows:

1   Students may be so relaxed and lacking in a useful sense of pressure that they do too little preparation, and are too casual about assessment. As a result they make errors of omission and, because they are not fully alert, miss deadlines or go for assessments unprepared.

If you recognise yourself in this group, you need to generate for yourself enough adrenaline to do your best in the assessment. Consider how best to do this both in the weeks beforehand, so you can gear yourself up for assessment by systematic preparation, and on the day, so you turn in a peak performance well above your normal best. It's a matter of channelling tension into a fast-paced and well-rehearsed performance.

2   Students may be generally anxious people. They may do particularly badly in significant assessments, and better in ones that do not count. The worry depresses their ability to revise and remember or to prepare adequately for an assessment. If they feel watched they may freeze up. If they do badly they believe it indicates their lack of ability, whereas more confident students are more likely to attribute a failure to lack of effort. They may tend to go over and over previous assessment work, looking for what they may have got wrong.

If you recognise yourself in this group bear in mind that anxiety does diminish when you begin to feel a grasp of some of the material. More people are afraid of having a complete mental block than actually suffer them. You should prepare for assessment early and systematically. I look at other techniques for managing anxiety later in this unit.

3   Students may have had a bad experience in one assessment and have anxiety linked specifically to assessments, even though they are not generally anxious.

If you recognise yourself in this group, you need to regain your confidence and optimism. One way to do this is to develop more realistic expectations of yourself. I discussed this in Unit 8: 'Coping with Perfectionism'. Another is to use your imagination to get used to coping with the specific fears the exam room holds for you. I look at exam anxiety, in particular, near the end of this unit.

Whichever of these groups you feel you most belong to, it is useful to identify your inner voice, and adapt it. For example, the 'I'm bound to fail' worrier could substitute more encouraging phrases; whereas the 'It'll be all right on the day' student may need to learn to add 'if I work systematically meanwhile'.

Overcoming panic

There are some symptoms which you should take seriously as signals that you could benefit from professional help in the weeks before your assessment.

I would suggest you seek professional help if you have more than one of these physical symptoms:

- feeling sick and going off food for weeks before;
- major and frequent sleep disturbances;
- headaches;
- inability to concentrate;
- poor short-term memory;
- fears for months of 'not having done enough' without taking action to retrieve the situation.

One student who suffered quite extremely wrote to me:

> I went though hell: nightmares of steamrollers crushing me, bluebottles attacking me. I had dreadful headaches, couldn't sleep and had blurring of the eyes. I went to the doctor who sent me to the hospital for tests, but they proved negative. The symptoms almost all went after the exams, though it took me three days to open the envelope with the results. I passed.

Panic in an assessment

As in most performances, panic in an assessment is usually focused immediately beforehand and at the point of starting. The panic can take many forms, for example, trembling or momentary speechlessness for people speaking in front of an audience, and difficulties with reading or understanding the question for people sitting an exam. This is how one person described the panic she feels in an exam:

> On the day I'm calm till I get there, then I start shaking; my mind goes blank; I start sweating; but once I see a question I can do I get a certain amount of recall, and then it gets better. The hardest part is getting going.

Most exam students who panic report that once they get under way they can regain some control. Thus their capacity to pass may depend on how quickly they can regain control and begin to work.

Managing anxiety

Here are some techniques for managing your own anxiety:

Use humour

Humour can help as you prepare, so you do not feel so caught up in the distress. One student remembered, during an exam-panic relaxation session:

> *When I was at childbirth practice the midwife actually said: 'Now the contractions are very painful - smile!' Perhaps laughing about it is a good idea. If I go in expecting to enjoy it, perhaps I could!*

Some exaggeration of the more obviously unhelpful fears can make it clear just how unrealistic they are, and a bit of humour can defuse them and reduce your anxiety about them.

Actively boost your self-confidence

Notice what you do effectively in other areas of your life. This can serve as a useful reminder that you are competent, and you can transfer some of this competence into your assessment work and preparation for assessment.

For example, planning to get a child a pair of new shoes involves advance thinking similar to the sort you need for revising. So does collating information about where to go for a holiday.

 Think about the time you first felt anxiety about assessment. Consider what has changed since then in terms of your ability to cope with demanding situations. For example, you are likely to be older and more resourceful. You may need to become aware of new resources that you haven't noticed because you are in the habit of expecting assessment to be traumatic.

Learn to relax

For any type of stress, including severe anxiety about assessment, it is worth learning some relaxation techniques that work for you. Your doctor may be able to recommend techniques, or you could try transcendental meditation or a local Yoga group. There are also relaxation tapes available, some of which are specifically designed to help reduce exam panic. (See Further Resources.)

Ideally, the best time to begin learning and practising relaxation is at least three months before an assessment. If you learn some techniques, and then practise them daily for no more than 15–20 minutes daily for three months, you will gain confidence that you will be able to control your anxiety, both generally and during an assessment, whether it is a demonstration, an oral test or an exam.

Learn to monitor your own tension level, and to identify where in your body you usually feel tension. Common symptoms are:

■ discomfort in the stomach;

■ headache or tight jaw;

■ knots in the back and neck.

Predict when you may be anxious, and begin practising your relaxation techniques immediately.

If you suffer from severe panic attacks you may find relaxation combined with visualisation particularly helpful. (See overleaf.)

Use a relaxation technique during assessment

During an assessment it is essential to interrupt the rise of panic as it begins. Otherwise, if you allow yourself to become very anxious, it can take up to twenty minutes to calm down. Practise calming techniques to use when you are being assessed. Here are two simple suggestions:

1   Take two or three deep breaths, relaxing and dropping your shoulders with a (quiet) sigh. Shut your eyes for a moment and picture someone who loves you saying something encouraging. Open your eyes and get on with the task.

2   As you become aware of your tension rising say firmly to yourself: 'STOP!' Take a few breaths and see if you have reversed the rising tension level.

Visualisation

Identify aspects of assessment that cause you to panic, and which will affect your performance in the assessment. Then aim to tackle these by yourself or with a counsellor. Relax, and visualise yourself overcoming the least fearful first, and then the others one at a time, until you can picture yourself doing an assessment confidently.

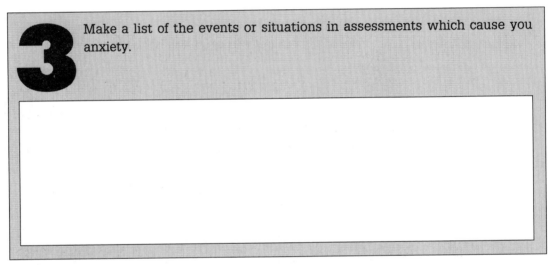

Make a list of the events or situations in assessments which cause you anxiety.

One student made the following list of possible events connected with an exam that made him panic. He ranked them in order, with the most fearful events first.

1   turning over the exam paper;

2   the invigilator not letting me go to the toilet;

3   not sleeping well because of having nightmares beforehand;

4   waiting to go into the exam room;

5   travelling there on the day of the exam;

6   another student asking for more writing paper;

7   discovering the night before a pile of notes I haven't looked at;

8   the invigilator saying 'Only five more minutes';

9   doing a mock exam;

10   the exam room.

As he worked up his list, imagining each until it held fewer fears, his capacity to prepare for his exam improved considerably.

Prepare early for the assessment

It is worth beginning your preparation early. See Units 5 and 10 on planning for assessment and revising for exams. Get support from a friend, relative or other student for testing and confirming what you can do.

Train yourself to start an answer

If your assessment involves an exam or an oral question-and-answer session, train yourself in the technique of starting an answer.

For example, for a written exam start with a blank piece of paper, a new question and a ten-minute time limit, feel the pressure of it, and then start planning your answer and writing your introductory paragraph. Keep doing this till you've developed the habit of 'instant planning'.

This is like building up a well-rehearsed routine for a show. You can do it automatically if you have drilled yourself sufficiently. Then you can polish the product. Because so many students who suffer from panic in an exam are most anxious at the point of planning their answer, this is a particularly useful technique for them, though it is useful for all people being assessed.

Find a model

Ask other students who do well in assessments how they tackle them. See if there are any elements in their way of approaching them that you would like to try. Using someone successful as a model is a well-established technique for athletes, and can work for people working towards assessment as well, particularly if you don't feel self-confident.

Another form of visualisation involves a model. Imagine what a person who succeeds in your assessment will be like. How do you feel about them? If your picture is of someone whom you would not want to be like, you should ask around to find or think of more likeable models.

If you see yourself as a 'victim' or 'dunce', consider what you would have to change about yourself to picture yourself as successful.

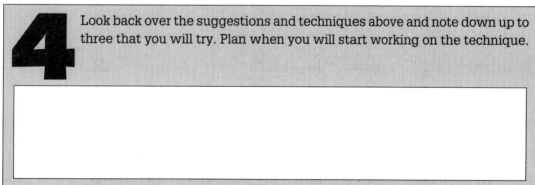

Look back over the suggestions and techniques above and note down up to three that you will try. Plan when you will start working on the technique.

When you have tried the ones you have identified, you may like to come back to this unit to review the techniques and try others.

Summary

In this unit you have seen that although some assessment anxiety is normal and helps your produce your best performance, high levels of anxiety can interfere with your performance. You have explored your own levels of anxiety and looked at a number of techniques for tackling anxiety. You should now be able to draw up a plan for implementing some of them.

UNIT 10

REVISING FOR EXAMS

What this unit is about

This unit focuses on preparation for written examinations, and looks at some of the skills and knowledge you need to develop to do yourself justice.

By the time you finish your work on this unit you should be able to:

➜ explain the structure of the exam you will be taking;

➜ make a revision timetable which takes into account the differing tasks of revision and your need for rest.

As part of your work on this unit I will encourage you to look at the syllabus for your course, or at past exam papers (or specimen papers if the course is new). If you have not yet done so you may wish to write away for these now.

The exam game

Exams are opportunities for a large number of people to be tested simultaneously about material they are expected to know and understand. Rather like games, they have their own rationale and rules, an understanding of which can enable you to revise effectively.

For most of the exams after GCSE more marks are given for applying the ideas in the course than for remembering them, so it is essential to spend revision time developing your ideas, linking ideas from different parts of the course, and identifying good examples under particular headings. At GCSE the balance is different, and much of your effort has to go into learning information. In either case the examiner has a marking scheme to work to and your job is to offer what will collect the marks. It may be hard to believe that the examiner wants you to do well, but it is usually true.

The process of revision

Most revision involves:

1   managing your allocation of time for revision and practice to prepare yourself for peak performance on the day.

2   rehearsing and feeling competent at answering the types of question which you will see in an exam;

3   developing your understanding of the essential information so that you feel comfortable and confident about demonstrating your knowledge and skills.

You therefore need to build two different sorts of task into your revision planning:

1 familiarising yourself thoroughly with your notes by condensing, memorising, and restructuring them;

2 using this increasingly solid base of information to answer questions, or plan skeleton answers.

I will look at both these tasks in more detail shortly. First, however, I want to make some general points about revision.

Ways of approaching revision

There are as many different ways of approaching revision as there are students, and you will need to experiment to discover what works for you.

What all approaches have in common, however, is the necessity to plan just as you would in preparing for any taxing test of your knowledge, capacity to think on your feet, and endurance under pressure. It is not sufficient to re-read old notes or course materials. You need to work always with a pen in your hand, actively condensing notes, jotting down new thoughts, and planning or preparing answers.

1 Recall the last exam you entered:

■ When did you begin your revision?

■ What helped you to feel confident and ready to work at your peak?

■ What hindered you in this?

Make brief notes in answer to these questions. Then read on and compare the advice in this section with your previous approach. I will be giving you plenty of useful hints, but in the end the points that will really help will be those that match your own experience; so take special note of the places where my suggestions and your ideas coincide.

When should I revise?

Ideally you will have discovered during your course when your most effective time to study is (this may not be the same as the most convenient one!). The more alert you are the more effective you will be. It is important to schedule your key revision tasks for this time of day, and do routine tasks at other times.

If you have not already discovered your ideal revision period, use the following SAQ to help you do so.

2 Look at your diary for the revision period or next six weeks and identify how many hours you have free to revise. See if there can be a regular time of day in this period. Possibilities include:

■ early morning, before work, college or household chores;

■ journeying to and from work or college;

■ at home during the day (if you have young children this may require special arrangements);

(continued opposite)

- ■ at work or college during the day (provided you can take tea or lunch breaks without fear of interruption);
- ■ at lunch time;
- ■ only or mainly at weekends;
- ■ during holidays or a period of study leave.

Make a note of these times below. You'll be able to use these in your revision plan, which I ask you to draw up in SAQ 4.

Where should I revise?

Ideally you will revise in a quiet, well-lit place where you can leave your study materials out, keep your timetable pinned up in good view, and feel at a comfortable temperature to work. You do need a desk or table to encourage you to do your revision actively. If you do not have such a space freely available, see if you can negotiate with others in your household for any work space where your materials can stay ready to hand, or find some orderly way to store them between work sessions so you waste the minimum of time searching for books and papers. If there is nowhere suitable at home, you may like to try to get a regular place in a library, so you begin to associate sitting down there with getting going on your studies.

Finding out about the exam

3 Make sure your revision plan is geared to the structure and focus of the exam. Use this SAQ as a systematic checklist.

Find your copy of the syllabus, a recent exam paper or specimen, and check the following:

- ■ How long is the exam?

- ■ How many questions do you have to answer?

(continued overleaf)

■ Will any of the assessment be based on:

   –   multiple-choice questions? ☐

   –   questions requiring short answers? ☐

   –   practical assessment? If so, what form does it take?

   –   oral assessment? If so, what are you expected to be able to do in it?

■ Are there requirements to complete any part at the start? Or can you choose the order and timing yourself?

■ Can you take in books? or a calculator? or a dictionary?

■ Will there be any compulsory questions? If so, has your course covered all that you need to know in order to tackle these?

■ Will you be given the exam questions in advance?

■ Are there topics which you might leave out?

■ Are questions written in such a way that you need to have a knowledge of more than one section of the course to answer them?

Finally, check the 'assessment objectives', which should be printed in a syllabus document or course guide.

Drawing up your final plan

You should now be in a position to make your revision plan, based on:

■ the information you have collected;

■ your tutor's advice on how much of the course you need to revise,

Bear in mind that any revision plan needs to be realistic. It needs to take into account:

■ other regular commitments in your life;

■ possible demands on your time in the revision period;

■ time for sociability and rest.

Otherwise you will only stick to it at a cost of becoming extremely inefficient during the hours you spend. It is far better to do fewer hours with clear aims than to spend all your available time languishing in front of your books without a sense of achievement for each hour of work.

4 Now draw up a timetable for revision. This can be in fairly general terms to start with. For a course lasting one year it should cover the last six to seven weeks, spent roughly as follows:

Four to five weeks: sorting notes and learning activities.

Final two or three weeks: practising answers.

Assign each of your main topics of study to a specific period. Then for each period of study set yourself a realistic objective (eg review topic X by answering question Y on the specimen exam). Your plan will feel more manageable if you have broken it down into specific objectives, and you will have the satisfaction of ticking off the goals as you complete them.

Allow yourself a week to ten days to try out your plan, and then review how you fared. You may then want to go into more detail, while still allowing time for reviews and adjustments as your work progresses.

Use a diary format to clarify exactly how you will fit in your revision. You could complete the outline on the next page, or use it as a guide (I'll say more about the final column in a moment):

For a less demanding course (eg a first-aid certificate) your plan could be more informal, for example:

Revise Tuesday

Practise Thursday

Discuss with course group Friday

Assessment Monday

Revision Plan

Week	Topics	Objectives	Treats!
1			
2			
3			
4			
5			
6			
7			

Taking breaks

During any period of revision it is vital, in order to stay alert, to take a break after every hour or so of work . You may find it useful to have a variety of treats to give yourself at these breaks: food, social contact, refreshment of any of your senses (listen to a tape, look at what is growing in the garden, eat, put supper in the oven and enjoy the aroma, have a hug). If you always use cups of tea and coffee or chocolate as rewards you will lose concentration (too much caffeine tends to depress the effectiveness of short-term memory) or run the risk of putting on a lot of weight!

5 If you have not done so already, add to your timetable specific plans for a day off from revision per week.

Consider how you will use this day. Your aim should be to rest and get a complete break from brainwork. For example, you could:

- go on an outing;

- do something physical even if it is housework;

- listen to music;

- spend time with someone who likes you.

Revising for resits

Check what you believe about why people fail exams. Does it mean the person is a failure? For many people, it does feel that way. But research shows that of those students who have passed on coursework, relatively few fail exams because they are stupid or inadequate. A high proportion can pass at a second attempt if they take appropriate action to:

- improve their exam technique;

- improve their capacity to cope with exam anxiety;

- reduce pressures on their time, capacity to concentrate, and feelings of self-esteem.

So if you have failed an exam and are re-taking it, take heart. Think that although you didn't get it right THEN it is possible with some work and support to get a different result NOW.

If you are planning to re-sit an exam, do not spend time going over the exam paper you failed, as the questions will not usually be asked in the same way a second time. Instead, make sure you use revision time to rebuild your memory of course ideas and facts; and if possible, do a mock exam and get feedback on your approach, so you have a better chance of passing this time.

Your confidence is likely to have been knocked by the failure so it is particularly important to read the sections on coping with panic, and building your self-confidence about being assessed.

Summary

In this unit I have explained the essential features of a revision plan. Use these ideas to decide when to begin your revision and to revise in an active way. I hope you will now appreciate how important it is to choose a time and place most suited to effective revision, and to allow yourself time to relax and socialise.

UNIT 11

PRACTISING FOR YOUR EXAM

What this unit is about

This unit continues the theme of the previous one. Although it is mainly about exams, it is also relevant to preparing for continuous assessment. This applies particularly to the advice on note-taking and planning answers.

By the time you have finished your work on this unit you should be able to:

→ use your notes as a revision tool;

→ recall information effectively;

→ plan your answers to exam questions;

→ practise writing answers to exam questions;

→ tackle a complete mock exam.

Spring-cleaning your notes

You may find it helpful to do the equivalent of a spring clean of your notes, handouts, photocopies, and other material. This can enable you to see:

■ overlaps between the different topics you have studied;

■ which topics you have covered in detail;

■ which topics have only sketchy coverage.

Where your notes are sketchy, or contain gaps, you will have to do some sustained work to review the course material, unless you have an excellent memory.

You may feel reluctant to review topics of least interest to you. If so, check with your tutor how crucial they are. If they are not, direct your energy elsewhere. If they are essential, make sure you tackle them early on and get support from the tutor or another student who understands and can help you to work on the material. Don't struggle on your own if you feel daunted. Get help!

Extending and improving your notes

Good note-taking should reflect the purpose for which the notes will be used. Revision notes are an aid to memory, and a way of condensing a substantial amount of material into a form which you can readily recall in an exam.

Simply reading your notes over and over again will not help you to understand them, nor is it a helpful way to memorise the key points. Successful learning and memorising of material involves three stages: understanding, storing and recalling. You can:

■ make summaries, condensing material from several sources;

■ select and memorise key ideas and vivid examples;

■ make lists of key words or definitions which will remind you of complex arguments;

■ rewrite material in your own words, where you have not already done so;

■ select and memorise quotable quotes.

You may find it helpful to use index cards as an aid to active revision. They can be a handy means of summarising notes, planning answers or noting down key themes and then practising your recall of them. This last point is worth considering in more detail.

Practising recall

It is useful to be aware of the way your memory works best. If your memory is visually strong you may find it helpful to practise visualising pages of your notes. You might be able to imagine bringing a specific part of a page into focus, or putting it in bold, or into colour if it is in black and white.

If your memory is stronger when you hear speech than when you read, you may be able to practise 'hearing' your tutor's voice telling you about a topic. Or you could revise by making yourself audio tapes of your key notes and playing them to yourself as you drive, iron or cook.

Or perhaps your memories tend to be linked to what else is happening at the time. For example, if you read about a topic on a bus journey you may be able to recall details by bringing to mind places you passed through. If this is useful to you, make a habit of asking yourself, 'What was happening when I was learning about this?'

Recalling during the exam

Many students find that one of the most frustrating points in an exam is when they feel something is 'on the tip of their tongue' yet are unable to think of it. But this need never happen! The trick is simply to search for thoughts or information related in some way to the 'lost' item. The next SAQ gives you the chance to try this out.

1 Try to recall what you had for supper last night.

When your memory has come to mind, reflect on the process you went through to retrieve it. (If you found that it sprang to mind immediately, try the night before instead.)

The chances are that you worked through something like a series of questions. For the example of supper these might be:

■ What day was it yesterday?

■ Who was I with?

■ When did I eat?

■ What had just been happening?

Few people fail to retrieve their memory of yesterday's supper. But notice how much more difficult it is to recall what you had on the first Sunday of last month – unless it was a very special day for you. Memories fade if they are not deliberately fixed by our efforts. This is why it is so important to set a couple of hours aside each week all through your course for sorting and reviewing notes. It is also why rehearsal of what you have learned pays dividends in the week before an exam!

If, despite all your efforts, you just cannot recall the point you want, don't spend a lot of time on it. Instead, move on in your answer, leaving a gap in your writing. You will often find that the missing item springs into your mind when you are least expecting it, and you can then go back and fill in the gap you have left.

2 Think about what I have just said. Which is your strongest form of memory?

Note down below:

■ the way in which you remember most effectively;

■ two or three ways in which you could apply this in revising your own subject.

Working with others

All students can benefit greatly from working with other students, 'testing' each other, talking over what you believe to be the meaning of key terms, and so on. If you have a strong auditory memory this is a particularly successful way to do your revision. It has the extra bonus of mutual encouragement and support, and motivation. Knowing that you have undertaken to work with someone on a topic can keep you at your revision when sunshine or the urge to lie down and sleep beckons.

Thinking like an examiner

A key part of your revision strategy should be to review each section of your course from the standpoint of an examiner: 'If I were writing a question to test people's understanding of this topic, what would I ask?'

Once you have learned to look at course material in this way you can begin to develop questions yourself. These may be based on existing ones. For example, if the original question was:

How did Elizabeth II sustain the monarchy in 1992?

you might change it to:

> *Why did Elizabeth II sustain the monarchy in 1992?*

or

> *'Elizabeth II's attempt to sustain the monarchy in 1992 was fundamentally unsound.' Discuss.*

or

> *Evaluate the success of Elizabeth II in sustaining the monarchy in 1992.*

and so on.

There are other ways of practising thinking like an examiner. You could:

■ plan answers to exam questions (your own and ones from the old exam papers), and then look up the course material to see what else you might have included;

■ swap answers with another student and discuss each others' plans;

■ write complete answers to individual questions.

You may have a tutor who is willing to mark work done under exam conditions, but if not, either work with another student or use your resource materials (notes, books etc.) to mark your own work.

3 Make your initial revision plans now. Note down:

■ When in your revision timetable you will need to begin working with exam questions:

■ How you will try to think like an examiner. Will you:

– develop your own questions? ☐

– plan answers to questions? ☐

– swap plans with other students? ☐

– write up finished answers? ☐

■ Who can help you in this?

– your tutor? ☐

– other students? ☐

(continued opposite)

■   What other resources do you need?

Tackling a mock exam

Some students find it helpful to tackle a complete mock exam. However, it can be difficult to set aside the time for this, and you are highly unlikely to want to do so more than once. It is therefore important to schedule your mock exam for when you have completed enough revision to make it worthwhile, but soon enough for you to have revision time left to remedy errors and seek answers to gaps.

It's not essential for everyone to do a complete mock exam. Like a marathon runner, you need only practise regularly for about three-quarters of the distance, and the adrenaline flow will take you to the finishing post. However, if you regularly word-process your assignments, and never, under normal circumstances, write for three hours continuously, you do need to have at least one full practice.

Keeping tabs on your progress

Keep a diary, notebook, or checklist to monitor your progress against your timetable and plan. Use it for goal setting to plan ahead for revising each topic, and then note what you are achieving. If you get behind your schedule, take action to catch up early on by putting in more time, using your time more effectively, or deleting a topic you intended to cover.

Summary

In this unit I have looked at ways of practising for exams. I have emphasised the importance of making creative use of your notes and maximising the power of your memory. I have also suggested ways of looking at your work from the point of view of the assessor – and of using others to assist you in this.

UNIT 12

ANSWERING THE QUESTION

What this unit is about

This unit focuses on sharpening up your awareness of what an exam question is asking you to do. This is useful at two different points: when you are doing your revision, and want to practise preparing answers; and in an exam itself, when you need to show you can answer the question effectively.

By the time you finish your work on this unit you should be able to:

→ decide what an exam question is asking you to do, and how you will tackle it.

You will find it useful to have your specimen papers to hand for activities later in the unit.

Doing precisely what an examiner requires is what distinguishes the student who answers the question from the one who doesn't. You can develop your skill in this by becoming aware of:

■ the verb used in the question;

■ the concepts used in the question.

This unit looks at each in turn.

Key verbs

1 These are some of the most common verbs used in essay-style questions. See how many of them you can put a definition beside (don't worry too much about finding an exact form of words). Then check your suggestions against mine, which follow.

Analyse	
Compare	
Contrast	
Define	

(continued overleaf)

Describe	
Discuss	
Distinguish between	
Evaluate	
Examine	
Explain	
Explore	
Interpret	
Justify	
Outline	
Relate	
State	
Summarise	
Trace	

Here are my suggestions:

Analyse: *Break up into parts; investigate*

Compare: *Look for similarities and differences between; perhaps reach a conclusion about which is preferable*

Contrast: *Bring out the differences between*

Define: *Set down the meaning of a word or phrase*

Describe: *Give a detailed account of*

Discuss: *Investigate or examine by argument; sift and debate; give reasons for and against; also examine the implications*

Distinguish between: *Indicate the differences between*

Evaluate: *Give your judgement about the merit of theories or opinions; back your judgement by a discussion of evidence or reasoning involved*

Examine: *Look closely into*

Explain: *Make plain; interpret and account for; give reasons for*

Explore: *Examine thoroughly, consider from a variety of viewpoints*

Interpret: *Make clear and explicit; show the meaning of*

Justify: *Show adequate grounds for decisions and conclusions; answer the main objections likely to be made to them*

Outline: *Give the main features or general principles of a subject, omitting minor details and emphasising structure and interrelations*

Relate: *a Narrate — more usual in exams*

b Show how things are connected to each other, and to what extent they are alike or affect each other

State: *Present in brief, clear form*

Summarise: *Give a concise account of the chief points of a matter omitting details and examples*

Trace: *Follow the development or history of a topic from some point of origin.*

Now review your own collection of past exam papers.

1 Draw up a list of the key verbs used in the questions.

2 Make your own glossary detailing what they mean. If you are in any doubt, ask your tutor.

Once you have identified key verbs, it can be useful to construct questions on the lines of those in your exam paper, but substituting different phrases to see how this changes the way you tackle your response.

For example, if the original question was:

It has been claimed that the nuclear family is a universal feature of human societies. Assess the evidence for this claim.

You might change the final sentence to:

Summarise the evidence for this view.

---

or

Trace the development of the family in Britain to test the validity of this view.

---

or

Evaluate this view, comparing and contrasting the nuclear family in Britain in the 19th and the 20th centuries.

Key concepts

Underlining key ideas is a well-established way of reminding yourself to define and analyse these at the planning stage of producing your answer. What's more, the process of asking yourself questions about the meaning of the key ideas provides you with the beginnings of your answer. Here's an example. Suppose the question was:

> *John Major failed as European President because he could not take calculated risks. Do you agree?*

First you would have to decide whether he had 'failed', and what would be relevant evidence for failure. You might want to ask yourself:

- Did he fail 'completely', partially or not at all?

- Did any achievements survive and form the basis for later developments?

- Did he fail for different reasons from the one cited?

You might want to comment about the focus on his role as European President, and indicate some limits to his success in this role caused by other factors in current politics.

And you also have to debate his risk-taking:

- What is a calculated risk? Is it one in which you weigh up the chances of success and failure, and only act if the balance is clearly indicated?

- Could he trust to luck, and take uncalculated risks? Would this have been preferable?

Having asked yourself these questions you can progress to the detailed planning of your answer. Your next steps are to:

- sift your evidence;

- select what is most relevant for consideration under each subheading.

Then you can plan a structure for your answer which uses your ideas and states your considered view.

Try this out for a question on one of your papers.

1 Underline the key concepts.

2 Then for each one aim to compile a list of two or three questions aimed at clarifying its meaning.

Tackling specific sorts of question: some tips

Tackling calculations

- When asked to carry out calculations you should expect to make use, at some point in your answer, of all the information which is given to you in the question. If you get to the end and have not made use of a particular dimension, check back for a mistake or a gap in your computation.

- In calculation questions an important set of key words are those which specify the use of a particular method, eg 'show graphically'.

■ Make these instructions part of your revision glossary and make sure you know what you are expected to do.

■ Look out for connections. A very common style of question is one consisting of different parts which are closely connected. Each builds on the one before so that earlier work is highly relevant to the later parts.

■ If the question contains the phrase 'Hence show...' you must use your previous piece of information in your subsequent calculation.

■ Where appropriate, draw a sketch diagram; it can be a valuable aid in carrying out a calculation and prevent you from arriving at impossible answers.

■ Always label diagrams which a question has specifically asked for.

■ Give numerical answers to three decimal places or in standard units.

If you get an answer which you sense is quite wrong, state that you think you may have made a mistake somewhere, and give your ideas of the range that the right answer should fall within.

Tackling multiple-choice questions

Multiple-choice questions are usually constructed so that the wrong answers are not just randomly wrong. Each is designed to test for a particular kind of error. Similarly the correct answer is designed to show you have grasped a particular skill or understand a particular piece of knowledge.

Here are some strategies for tackling multiple-choice questions in an exam:

1 Go through the questions very quickly filling in any answers which are obvious to you, and which you are confident are correct.

2 Go back to the questions which required more thought and work through them systematically but not too slowly. Each carries so few marks it is not worth puzzling over them for long.

3 Decide whether to guess the answers for those which you are still uncertain about. Unless the marking scheme penalises you for wrong answers, which is fairly rare, it is worth guessing.

4 Allow more time afterwards to check back. Review the answers you were unsure about to see if you can work out what errors each might be testing for.

5 Keep a careful watch on your time.

Summary

In this unit you have explored ways of homing in on exactly what is being asked in an assessment question. I have explained that this is valuable both in revision and in the exam itself. You should now be able to approach assessment questions more confidently, with a sense of what ideas you are being asked to address, and how you should set about this.

UNIT 13 GETTING IT RIGHT ON THE DAY

What this unit is about

The final unit of this book tackles the all-important question of how you apply in an examination room the strategies you have learned beforehand.

By the time you finish your work on this unit you should be able to:

→   make practical arrangements for your exam;

→   decide on the approach you need to take in the exam.

Introduction

You have now done your preparation, and marshalled what you know onto summary sheets or cards, focused on typical questions. You have done most of your preparatory thinking by planning answers to practice questions. Now you need to trust that you will be able to use these strategies on the day. You will then be able to use your energy in the last few days to ensure that:

■   the practicalities go smoothly;

■   you fix key ideas firmly in your mind.

Let's consider the practicalities first.

Making practical arrangements

You should be able to make any administrative arrangements well in advance. Enrolment and registration dates for the exam are usually clear at the start of the course, together with instructions about any arrangements that you need to make for yourself.

However, you may need to make other arrangements because of your personal situation; for example, you may be employed, or responsible for dependants. Here are some of the additional questions you may need to address, depending on your circumstances.

If you are employed, ask yourself:

■   Am I allowed time off work for revision? Some employers have a policy of paid educational leave up to a week before particular exams. It can be worth asking.

■   Do I need to book time off in good time to accommodate rotas for shift work or to allow for busy periods?

If you work at home, paid or unpaid, ask yourself:

■   Can I arrange for some time off? If not, why not?

If you sometimes need to work away from home at short notice, ask yourself:

■ Do I need to check whether my exam board can arrange for exams to be taken at a special time? (Such arrangements may not be easy to make but it is worth enquiring.)

If you are looking after children or dependants, ask yourself:

■ Is there someone who could be with my children at home even if they are not well on the day?

If you are caring for someone with special needs, ask yourself:

■ Will the temporary carer need a practice visit so that I can guide them in what the recipient needs and prefers?

Use the table below to note down any special arrangements you need to make:

What I need:	Who can help:	When I will ask them by:

Preparing for the exam

Check the detailed arrangements at least one week beforehand.

■ Ensure you've got the right date, and know the location of the exam. If you are at all uncertain where it is, consider taking a trip there beforehand to establish how long the journey will take, and where the exam is located. If your practice trip is in the evening or at the weekend, look out for evidence that traffic flows might be slower on a weekday morning.

If there is a long journey to the exam, or your access to transport is difficult, you may decide to stay overnight before a morning exam. If so, ensure that you have booked your room in good time.

■ Check what supplies you need for the exam, and provide ones that are your favourites (eg a good pen or biro). If you buy new pens or other equipment, test them first to make sure that everything is in working order. If you are taking a calculator into the exam, take a spare battery.

■ Check whether you can take in a snack if you want one (not one with a noisy wrapper, of course!).

■ Check that you have all the necessary paperwork, such as your exam number and receipt.

Two final points

Would you find it comforting to take a small mascot? Some people really value them; others would not want to bother.

It can be useful to take a packet of tissues, and to dress in layers of loose comfortable clothing which can be adjusted however hot or cold the exam room turns out to be.

The morning of the exam

Imagine how you might like to prepare for the exam on the morning it is due. What do you know puts you in a calm and 'ready to go for it' mood? Spend five minutes noting down your ideas on a separate sheet before continuing.

My suggestions would include:

Get up early enough to give myself an unhurried start and if I can comfortably digest it, a breakfast to fuel me for the exam (Perhaps a treat? For me it would be a grapefruit and possibly toast and tea.)

Depending on weather and light, consider taking some sort of exercise to get my energy flowing: a brisk walk, even just around the block? Or perhaps even a swim or a run?

Spend some time with someone who is an ally, even if it is only via a brief phone call. Ideally this person needs to convey that they will continue to love me whether or not I pass, but that they have every confidence I will do myself justice!

Set off in good time so that you can get to the exam room without fear of travel delays. Spend the time you have in hand getting ready to start, perhaps by reviewing your summary notes just as a reminder of how much you DO know. Think of yourself as 'ticking over ready for the green light'. This means being alert for the signal to change, but using the space of the red light for a moment of relaxation, rather than revving the accelerator frantically for the fastest possible getaway! Take in any equipment you require, together with any necessary spares.

Exam tactics

Your first steps

Take into the exam room any paperwork, such as your exam number and receipts for fees you have paid.

Put bags or files of notes where the invigilator tells you to, and listen carefully for other instructions. Find your desk, and sit down. While others are settling, you have another opportunity for some brief relaxation. Most people will feel tense at this point, needing to get on and get going, or get it over with, depending on their mood. A few deep breaths and quiet sighs will release some of this tension, and ensure that you are ready to follow instructions to begin.

If specialist equipment should have been provided, check that it is all there. In the unlikely event that there is anything missing, ask for it immediately.

Getting started

Turn over the paper when the invigilator tells you to. Scan all the questions, looking for familiar words, phrases and concepts. Then look particularly closely at any questions on the topic areas you have revised most. From your findings, make a provisional decision about which questions you will answer.

Planning a question

Take your time to underline the key words, and check the verbs that tell you what to do (see Unit 12). Note whether the question asks you to do more that one thing. If so, plan accordingly.

Look for anything which is ambiguous, and make sure that you know and can define the meaning of any terms that you are going to use.

As you create a plan, remember the skills you have practised in recalling information (see Unit 11). Jot down relevant facts, names or evidence for your key points.

Make regular checks to ensure that you are planning to answer the question as set. One way of doing this is to ask yourself questions about the question. Read the question several times, putting emphasis on different words, and see if it makes a difference to your idea of what this is about.

Choosing 'easy' or 'difficult' questions

Students often ask me whether they can gain most marks by tackling 'safe' easy questions, which will be popular with many candidates, or more risky, difficult questions that fewer will attempt.

There are two good reasons why it may be worth your while to answer a more difficult question:

1   If it is answered by fewer students, or all students find it difficult, you may get a higher mark than for the easy ones.

2   As you plan your answer you may find your revision and interest in the topic stand you in good stead, and the question is actually more straightforward than it first appeared.

However, if you panic at unfamiliar questions, and there are easier alternatives, it may be best to avoid stirring yourself up. Alternatively, a good compromise is to steady yourself by tackling an easier question to start with and then reviewing your strategy as you feel some confidence returning.

Managing your time

It is vital to keep an eye on the time, and work within an overall timetable. Below I suggest three possible ways of planning your time. Whichever one you choose, you will need to monitor yourself to ensure that enough time remains to answer all the outstanding questions.

Plan A

Plan your answers to all the essay questions before you begin to write.

You may find this the best option if:

■   you are calm;

■   you feel you have revised thoroughly;

■   you have no worries about hearing other students writing busily around you.

This planning stage is potentially a great bonus, as you may be reminded of key points for one answer in the course of planning for another. The additional ideas, or even the shift in focus, can then be integrated seamlessly into the final work!

But you will need to be clear how much time to allocate to the planning, and not overrun this. A maximum would be about 40 minutes for a three-hour exam which required you to answer four questions.

Plan B

Choose the question about which you feel you have most confidence, and answer that. Once this one is under your belt and completed on time you may then either tackle each of the others in the same way, or settle down at that point to plan all the others.

You may prefer to follow this option if you are more anxious, or need to begin writing in order to build up confidence and do yourself justice.

Plan C

First pick an answer you can do adequately, and then save your best question to do second. You may be more likely to write your best answer second because by then you will have got into your stride, and found your rhythm.

For plans B or C it will be more important to leave time at the end of the exam to check over your entire script to see if small improvements can be made.

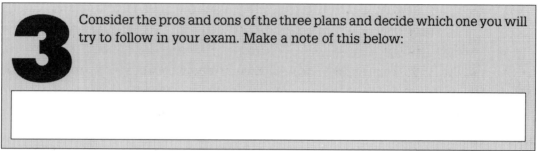

Consider the pros and cons of the three plans and decide which one you will try to follow in your exam. Make a note of this below:

You may find it difficult to decide which of the three plans is most appropriate for you. In this case you may find it helpful to tackle one or more mock exams to discover your preferred approach.

If things don't go according to plan

Running out of time

If you begin to run out of time, stop and re-plan the rest of the exam. Ask yourself:

- Could I manage to do a basic answer for all questions?
- Can I quickly finish the question I am currently working on?
- Could I be much more concise?
- Could I finish in skeleton note form, or show the relevant steps in a calculation even if I do not have time to carry them out?

Bear in mind that you must always answer the number of questions asked for. It will always be easier to gain a few quick marks for a new answer, even if it is very short or in note form, than to squeeze a few additional marks out of an answer which is already of a reasonable standard.

Panicking

If you can't get started, or lose your nerve in the middle, try one or more of the following:

1   Shut your eyes and take some deep breaths, sigh, allow yourself to picture someone who thinks you are OK; imagine their voice saying something encouraging.

2   If you panic because you are stuck with a question, leave it and work on your plan for the next one.

3   Go to the loo. You can feel much more relaxed just by getting out of the exam room for a few minutes.

4   Take a complete rest for three minutes, daydream, relax. Then sit up very straight so there is room to breathe deep into your lungs, and begin work again.

Presentation and layout

Lay out your work as simply as possible. Imagine a tired examiner reading the fiftieth answer to the same question. They need help to see easily what you mean. You can provide this by using:

■   short sentences;

■   separate paragraphs for each new point;

■   clear diagrams.

Focus your attention on quality of response more than on quantity. Provided that you say all that is necessary in order fully to answer the question, you are unlikely to gain additional marks for length.

It can be useful to leave a gap of several lines between paragraphs of an essay or at the end, so that when you come back to read it through you can insert any points which have occurred to you later, or, even more important, add in a sentence to make clear the relevance of the material in the paragraph.

Remember, too, that if you cannot recall a particular name, date, fact or quote, you can leave a space and trust your memory will find it when you take the pressure off. If it does not, you can still put in a word or phrase to refer to what's missing.

Looking after yourself

Allow yourself brief rests in the exam. Loosen up physically, stretch (if you can do so without feeling awkward), take several deeper breaths. If you need to think, use this as an opportunity to shut your eyes.

Avoiding perfectionism

Leave time to check and polish your answers at the very end, but avoid unnecessary perfectionism. The examiner knows that this is an exam answer and does not expect elegantly written prose, or striking originality. They will simply want to see whether you can understand a question and create a well-argued answer in a very short space of time. They cannot possibly assess all you know about a topic under these circumstances, and they do not expect to. So give yourself permission to do a competent job and get on with the task!

Summary

You have now considered the practical arrangements you need to make for your exam and then decided on what approach you need to take in the exam itself. I hope that you will now be able to enter the examination room with greater confidence, knowing that you will be able to apply some of the strategies that I have outlined here.

For your notes

Further Resources

Books

Managing exam anxiety:

Acres, David *How to Pass Exams Without Anxiety*, available from How to Books, Plymbridge House, Estover Road, Plymouth, PL6 7PZ Tel: (0752) 735251. This contains good advice on revision and anxiety management.

Davies, Don *Maximising Exam Performance: A Psychological Approach*, Kogan Page 1986. This book reports the result of a survey of stress related problems of post A level students, and suggests some ways to do the psychological preparation for exams.

General study skills:

Northedge, Andrew *The Good Study Guide*, Open University Press 1990. An excellent general resource about study skills aimed primarily at adult students.

A book that I have consulted and found particularly stimulating is:

Lloyd-Jones, B and Bray, E *Assessment: From Principles to Action*, Routledge 1992. This book is designed to help classroom teachers with assessment issues, and in it I found a very useful exploration of key concepts in assessment, and details about assessment techniques.

Audio tapes:

Many general relaxation tapes are available. Two specific to preparation for examinations are:

How to Conquer Exam Nerves: Maximising Examination Performance Don Davies. This 64-minute tape covers test anxiety; anxiety stress and performance; learning to relax; developing confidence; improving concentration and increasing efficiency. Available by post from Performance Programmes, 16a Priory Road, Malvern, Worcester WR14 3DR. Tel: (0684) 575798.

Relaxation Training Cassette Madeleine McGill, available from the Student Counselling Service, University of Technology, Loughborough, Leicester LE11 3TU.

Other books in this series

Clear Thinking

John Inglis and Roger Lewis

An invaluable book for anyone who wants to organise and express their thoughts more effectively, or to analyse the arguments of others. Particularly useful for students preparing for assessment, whether verbally or in writing. Topics covered include: propositions and arguments; assertions; abuses of argument; using source material; applying clear thinking to poetry, prose, and art.

How to Study Effectively

Richard Freeman and John Meed

Enables students to identify their own aims and needs, and to prepare an action plan for effective study. All the essential skills of reading, writing and assessment are fully covered in a practical and reassuring way. Topics include: analysing your learning style; identifying learning techniques; effective reading; note-making; writing; assessment; using additional resources.

How to Use Your Dictionary

Roger Lewis and Martin Pugmire

Shows how dictionaries can be used to assist at many stages of study, from clarifying meanings and spellings to finding out about pronunciation and the origins of words. Includes numerous examples from a wide range of dictionaries. Topics include: using a standard dictionary; finding meanings; finding spellings; pronunciation; checking the history of a word.

How to Write Essays

Roger Lewis

An ideal remedy for the blocks many students experience when it comes to essay writing. Covers all the stages of successful essay writing from rough notes to the final presentation, and includes hints on using the comments of friends and tutors. Invaluable for students at all levels, from GCSE to A level and beyond.

Acknowledgements

This book could not have been written without the help of many people:

The students who attended my Open University exam panic workshops in the 1980s and taught me about the issues of panic and perfectionism.

Many colleagues in the worlds of education and counselling, and the authors of previous NEC examination texts, especially Christopher Moor and Eddy Knasel.

My grown-up children who have survived years of examinations with their usual mixture of stress and aplomb, and Bob who gave me the space to write and the heart to complete it.

The editorial team – Tim Burton, Leslie Partridge and Pat McNeill – who have provided unique and sensitive support to meet very tight deadlines. Thank you all.

Penny Henderson

March 1993.

The publishers would like to thank the City and Guilds of London Institute for permission to quote from their Communication Skills (Wordpower) Scheme Pamphlet.